AF668364

A GRACIOUS VOICE

Life of Oommen Chandy

A GRACIOUS VOICE

Life of Oommen Chandy

P.T. Chacko • Dr. C.C. Thomas

KONARK

KONARK PUBLISHERS PVT LTD
NEW DELHI • SEATTLE

KONARK PUBLISHERS PVT LTD
206, First Floor, Peacock Lane,
Shahpur Jat, New Delhi-110 049.
Phone: +91-11-41055065, 65254972
E-mail: india@konarkpublishers.com
Website: www.konarkpublishers.com

Konark Publishers International
1507 Western Avenue, #605,
Seattle, WA 98101
Phone: (415) 409-9988
e-mail: us@konarkpublishers.com

Copyright © P.T. Chacko, 2011

All rights reserved. No part of this book may be reproduced or utilised in any form or by any means, electronic or mechanical, including photocopying, recording, or by any information storage and retrieval system, without prior permission in writing from the publisher.

Cataloging in Publication Data--DK
Courtesy: D.K. Agencies (P) Ltd. <docinfo@dkagencies.com>

Cākkō, Pi. Ṯṯi.t
A gracious voice : life of Oommen Chandy / P.T. Chacko, C.C. Thomas.
p. cm.

ISBN: 9788122007954

1. Ummancāṇṭi, 1943- 2. Politicians--India--Kerala--Biography.
I. Thomas, C. C., Dr., joint author. II. Title.

DDC 324.2092 22

Editor: Seema Sreenivas
Designed and Layout by Idesign, New Delhi-110 017
Printed at Lustra Print Process, New Delhi

Contents

Foreword

In 1978, when I started my career with the United Nations at Geneva as a young international civil servant, Sri Oommen Chandy was already into his second stint as a Member of the Kerala Legislative Assembly. By the time I left the UN 29 years later in 2007, Sri Chandy was still going strong into his ninth consecutive term in the legislature. By then he had become the tallest leader of the UDF coalition headed by his party, the Indian National Congress, in the Assembly of the State. The parliamentary constituency of the capital, Thiruvananthapuram, was from where, in the summer of 2009, I on my own part made my entry at my first attempt to the Lok Sabha, the apex house of the Indian democracy.

Sri Chandy's record of contesting nine straight elections and winning each one of them over a period spanning close to half a century, and that too from the same constituency, Puthupally, in Kottayam district, where he first contested as a 27 year-old, is a remarkable feat in the annals of Indian parliamentary democracy. All through this long career he never wavered in his belief in and commitment to, the party of his political birth, the Indian National Congress. In faithful service of the State, he has donned the roles of a humble foot solider as well as of the Chief Minister and the Leader of the Opposition, with equal felicity and dedication.

My entry into active politics in India and subsequent election to the Lok Sabha as a Congress candidate from the Thiruvanathapuram Parliamentary constituency was achieved in the background of the presence of luminaries of profound personal integrity such as Sri Oommen Chandy. Right from the very beginning he has never failed to shower me with his affection, guidance, and unstinted support. And to me he has always been OC *chettan*, an elder brother. This feeling of deep closeness has extended to my relations with his able son Sri Chandy Oommen, a fellow Stephanian who emulated me by being elected President of the College Union three decades after myself.

Whenever Sri Chandy shouldered important responsibilities in Government, he has never failed to prove his administrative acumen.

As a Minister in the State Cabinet and as the Chief Minister, his tenures were marked by notable achievements. His decision as Labour Minister to grant unemployment allowance to thousands of educated unemployed was truly historic. As Home Minister he instilled a sense of confidence, and gave a new look to the police force with an imaginative change in their uniform keeping in tune with the times. As Finance Minister, he never turned away from taking hard decisions to set the economy back on track and stabilise the state. His rather short but eventful stint as Chief Minister, from August 2004 to May 2006, was marked by the taking of decisive measures for the setting up of many developmental projects which are bearing fruit today. Special mention has to be made about the Smart City Project at Kochi which showed his deep commitment to the development of IT in the state. The 320 crores Master Plan for the famous Sabarimala shrine complex and a 356 crores Pampa Action Plan, which, if had been carried forward to their logical conclusion by the successor LDF government, could well have prevented the horrific tragedy that occurred there very recently, which led to the loss of over hundred precious lives, all innocent pilgrims.

The story of Sri Oommen Chandy's life contains many more elements which are strikingly inspirational. The great value of this rather slim but enlightening biography of the man, is in the details it provides of these extra facets of his life and personality. To the uninitiated, the contents of this book will offer a profitable revelation of the better side of Indian politics which is the undoubted backbone of Indian democracy, a still unexplained enigma to the outside world.

This little volume contains an absolute wealth of narration, replete as it is with accounts of incidents, many of them humorous to the point of being simply hilarious in their very innocence, reflecting the essence of the man and his approach to the people who are his very life. These incidents bring to vivid focus his urge to be always with the people, his 24x7 work schedule, his compassion for those in trouble, his willingness to make the extra effort for all those who may benefit from it, his frankness in dealing with friends and opponents, openness in personal behaviour bordering on carelessness towards personal appearance, willingness to sacrifice almost every ounce of privacy so that others may not feel discomfited or waste their time and effort (which results in total accessibility to almost every individual), and the almost unfathomable depth of his personal relationship with his constituency of Puthupally, and very much more.

Story after story is narrated here without striking a single note of falsehood, or leaving any trace of ambiguity about the various aspects of his admirable character. When he held office as the Chief Minister, his chamber was kept open to the world via his website, an act which prompted former President of India, Sri A. P. J. Abdul Kalam, himself one of the most open of men, to send a letter of appreciation. Every movement in the room was transmitted, moment by moment, to the world outside through the web camera–a virtual live telecast of what is normally treated in every such office in India, as a sacrosanct private fortress of administrative power. The crowd was his strength and he never felt right when he was removed from them. An incident is narrated about when he had to be admitted to the ICU of a hospital after a major fracture to his leg. He could not bear the loneliness even for a few hours and insisted on being shifted to a ward so that he could be surrounded by the people who wanted to see him. At the time of his marriage, he was so busy that the engagement ceremony was conducted without him. He does not have the patience or time to have a proper haircut. His wife cuts his hair. Once he landed up at his house at an unexpected hour and found that there was nothing to eat. His wife was away and he did not want to send his gunman to get some food from outside. A further search revealed two rotting bananas which his wife had kept aside for their pet parrot. He quietly ate them and went to sleep!

His 24x7 work schedule is the stuff of legend. It gives him an unmatched air of omnipresence which is one of the most valuable traits that a leader of men can and should possess. A journalist acquaintance of mine once narrated to me an incident (not described in the book) which distinctively brings to light this attribute of the man. Once this journalist's brother, a government official, was taken into police custody late in the night for failing to report for election duty. The brother could not attend to his election duty only because he had fallen ill suddenly, but that did not save him from a mindless arrest. On being informed about his brother's arrest, the journalist frantically tried to get through to the District Collector; but he could not since it was by then an hour past midnight. As a last resort he tried Sri Oommen Chandy's number. To his surprise, the phone was answered by the Chief Minister himself! Sri Oommen Chandy immediately called up the Collector, and the latter reached the police station concerned within half-an-hour and had the journalist's brother released from custody.

This is undoubtedly Sri Oommen Chandy's story, and what a story it is. No effort has been made to buffer facts or provide unnecessary details. Each narration reveals without too many frills an important prospect of his personality. Many of these stories are already legend among political workers and the public in the state. But they truly deserve to be known by a much wider audience in the country. I am sure that this book will serve to fill that need to a great extent.

This age of cynicism about politics and politicians calls for the tempering solace of glimpses into the lives and work of persons like Sri Oommen Chandy. Fortunately, the story is still incomplete, and still more significant achievements await him. To know the story so far and grasp its essence, will serve as a timely and effective cleansing of the negative emotions of pity and fear, which seem to dominate the general thinking about politics in our country today.

This is a story which deserves to be widely known among all well-wishers and participants of Indian democracy. I am delighted to commend it to what I hope will be a large and discerning readership.

Dr Shashi Tharoor
Member of Parliament (Lok Sabha),
Noted author and columnist

Part One

CHAPTER ONE

To Oppose And To Assist

A man came with a milch cow to OC, as Oommen Chandy is called by his close associates. He had a unique complaint to lodge. It did not bother him that, as Leader of the Opposition of Kerala, OC had more important things to do. The matter had to do with a breach of promise. He had bought the cow after being assured of seven litres of milk but the poor mammal could yield only three. If OC did not believe him, he could visit him and witness the sorry spectacle himself. OC, however, resolved the issue amicably at once. This was but one of the numerous disputes that OC has had to settle for people who throng around him wherever he goes.

On 18 May 2006, OC became the Leader of the Opposition of the Kerala Legislative Assembly. It came after his short tenure as the state's chief minister. His style of functioning, habits, hard work, and close association with the people at large, remained much the same. Whether in power or out of power, OC has always related to the people of the state.

As Opposition Leader he has known only restless days and sleepless nights. The ruling Left Front has provided enough material for OC's insomnia. He has been closely observing every move of the government, weighing and considering what suits the state and what does not. He sharpens his responses and shapes his policies accordingly. To fight the government, he has resorted less to the wonted ways of bundhs, hartals, and strikes, and has taken more to real democratic methods. He rushes to wherever problems crop up, consoles the victims and inspires the dispirited people there.

'All-Round Development' is OC's war cry for Kerala. And development is precisely what has remained almost at standstill in the state. Intramural rivalries and squabbles have incapacitated the government in several instances. Considering the pros and cons of the post-2006 LDF performance in Kerala, OC's verdict has been simply put in two words—'Wasted years.'

The Opposition Leader's line of action has been decidedly constructive. He has carved out for himself a Gandhian ideology in order to fashion his political framework. He is not in favour of violent demonstrations to let off steam but will instead, endorse a carefully planked democratic, secular action plan for the welfare of the nation. OC would heartily expend himself in the service of the state by visiting places, meeting people, conferring with the media and setting down his strongly worded queries and inquiries, replies and responses, retorts and reactions.

Almost none of the initiatives taken during the previous UDF regimes, led by A. K. Antony and OC, were continued by the LDF government. Development has nearly come to a grinding halt in this part of the country which has one of the highest potential for growth: 'Vision 2010'; a much lauded programme, conceived by former President A. P. J. Abdul Kalam, was the first to be dumped. The Smart City Project has taken off only recently after years of dilly-dallying. The Vizhinjam Harbour Project can also be treated as a casualty. The Cochin Metro plan is likely to be derailed. The Vallarpadam Project is, thankfully, a central government scheme, though the state government has been entrusted with the acquisition of land for road and rail connectivity. But it progressed at a snail's pace. The social security measures, such as Health Insurance and *Ashraya* Scheme, have been thwarted. The investment index of India shows that Kerala is close to the bottom. Kerala tops the nation now in social evils, like higher level of alchohol consumption, lottery, suicides, crimes, road accidents, and so on. 'Kerala Fast Backward' seems to be a more fitting slogan for the present.

When the United Democratic Front (UDF) occupied the ruling benches in 2001–2006, the Left Democratic Front (LDF) sponsored 22 bundhs in the state. Now, in spite of the many oppressive ways of the government, the UDF has resorted to hartals only twice during 2006–2011 while the ruling LDF themselves went in for 12 of them during this period. This is the sad story of Kerala which touts itself as 'Gods Own Country'!

Innumerable cases of injustice and indifference have caught OC's attention. As Opposition Leader, he has been taking firm action against all of them. He has been against bundhs and hartals except in extraordinary circumstances. Non-violent measures have always inspired him. His offensive arsenal contains speeches, letters, and articles; strikes and demonstrations; fasts and marches. These are enough for him to fight the good fight.

Another example of his willingness to be flexible in his fight against the injustices of the government was when Chickungunya spread like wildfire in 2007, and many died, and many more were hospitalised. The government did not respond or act in a swift enough manner. The UDF called for a bundh. People from all quarters asked him to cancel it, and OC graciously obliged. He, instead, went on a 24-hour fast in front of the Secretariat in Trivandrum to protest against the government's paralysis in fighting the contagion. He also fasted at Pathanamthitta, to express his solidarity with the running strike undertaken by the dalits and tribals on Chengara Estate. When the BJP and the CPM violently clashed in Kannur, he again fasted there, for a rapid return to peace in that region. The UDF resorted to bundhs only on two extreme occasions and only because their other weapons failed. The first was when the prices of essential commodities were shooting up unbearably. The second was when the government failed to give prosecution sanction against the culprits in the Lavalin case.

OC says that he has turned to writing because he is forced to write letters to the CM and the ministers on many an issue that keeps cropping up day after day. The Left Front has made him a 'writer'! Issues and debates are present by the score, and more. OC has been spearheading the offensive on behalf of the UDF. He has indeed proved that the pen is mightier than bundhs and hartals in political battles.

The Chengara Strike

One of the biggest achievements of OC as Opposition Leader was his intervention in settling the 795-days old agitation led by a large group of dalits, tribals and others under the banner of *Sadhujana Vimochana Samyuktha Vedi* for land at Chengara in Pathanamthitta district. Under the terms of the settlement, 1,432 of the 1,738 families who had occupied land belonging to Harrison's plantation in Chengara would be given land and assistance to build houses. The others, who already owned more than five cents of land, would get help to construct houses. The decision was reached at the meeting convened by Chief Minister V. S. Achuthanandan (or VS, as he is popularly called). OC was the driving force behind the agreement and it was arrived at in accordance with his formula. It was, of course, surprising for everybody that on 5 October 2009, the agitation was called off on the Opposition Leader's terms and conditions.

The Chengara strike needs special mention. Men and women, young and the old alike, had taken shelter in the ramshackle dwellings built on the estate. They defied the heat and the cold, all for a shelter of their own. Thirteen of them breathed their last there, having been unable to bear the hardships. Seventeen marriages took place and nine newborns also called it their home. All this and more happened during the prolonged occupation.

OC had wholeheartedly supported the move. During his visit on 25 September 2008, he was very affected by the miseries of the hapless people, and wrote the CM a series of letters on the issue, stating ways and means of settling the strike. He requested the CM to visit the place and urged for an amicable settlement in the matter. The government did not. OC went on a hunger strike in March 2009. In the assembly sessions too,

OC had constantly raised the Chengara issue. The Chengara settlement is definitely a golden moment in OC's distinguished political career.

The Lavalin Case

The SNC Lavalin deal is one of the most scandalous corruption charges that independent India has so far witnessed. The then Power Minister Pinarayi Vijayan, the State Secretary of the CPM, is suspected to be the kingpin in this shady affair. The CPM believes that he has been unnecessarily implicated in the case to malign him and the party. The UDF, on the other hand, is urging the accused to undergo a judicial trial.

The gigantic loss in the Lavalin deal was first pointed out in the Comptroller and Auditor General's report. The then UDF government had referred the case to the CBI. The LDF-led government insisted that the central agency should not deal with it. A plea in public interest was taken up by the High Court. The government spent lakhs in legal fees to avoid a CBI enquiry in the matter. The High Court maintained that the case should be left to the CBI.

The Lavalin issue took the Assembly by storm. OC has been leading the war against the same, both inside and outside the House. When the Advocate General gave his legal advice that there was no prima facie case against the accused, and the government endorsed it and forwarded it to the governor, the UDF rose in righteous fury. That resulted in an immediate call for a bundh. OC urged the government and the governor to give consent to the prosecution procedure against the accused. The CBI also applied for the same. Governor R. S. Gawai gave his sanction and he suddenly became the pivot of debate. His decision made headlines in the national media. Gawai's observation will always be a point of reference when there is any attempt to cover up corruption in high places. Whether the governor can override the decision of the Cabinet, is a constitutional question which will be hotly discussed in the days to come.

There were two objections in the Lavalin affair. The first was that the expected procedures were not observed and that an international tender was not called for when the Canadian company, SNC Lavalin, was contracted to do the renovation works at the Panniyar, Pallivasal, and Chenkulam hydro-electric projects. The renovation work was done at an exorbitant rate; and it was a complete waste of money and not up to standards. The Government of Kerala incurred a loss to the tune of 374.5 cores, according to the report of the CAG. Along with the renovation works, Lavalin was to give 98.30 crores for the Malabar Cancer Care Centre at Thalassery. The second objection was that the Cancer Centre did not get the duly paid up amount of 89.32 crores of the promised amount.

Smart City

OC, as Chief Minister, had initiated the Smart City project for greater growth in the Kerala IT sector. Smart City was his 'IT Baby'. The Left parties, especially the then opposition leader V. S. Achuthanandan, had opposed it in every way possible. VS even threatened to put OC behind bars. The moment the LDF came to power, VS himself encouraged the Smart City project, offering more concessions than the UDF had done. Inspite of this, OC was supportive of their moves but, exposed the loopholes in the agreement that was signed at the fag end of the LDF Governemnt.

Dubai Internet City, a Dubai-based firm, was to invest 2,000 crores in Smart City, Cochin; it was a welcome relief to the animosity towards private enterprise in Kerala. As CM, OC had made his first foreign trip to Dubai. During this visit he had called on the Internet City headquarters. The CM had invited the opposition MLAs accompanying him to join him for the visit, but they had refused. The opposition then arraigned the UDF Government of gross corruption in the deal. OC knew that his hands were clean; he could undertake the venture without any prick of conscience.

He had held talks on more than one occasion with the Opposition on the Smart City project. During the discussions, VS fought the project outright. Thomas Isaac, another representative of the CPM, pointed out that they were not against the arrival of Smart City; but that the party was against letting go of the Info Park, Cochin, the 2nd IT Park developed by the Government of Kerala in 2004 after Technopark in Trivandrum. Isaac's stand enabled the government to go ahead with it. OC could have made the final agreement with Dubai Internet City on Smart City on the eve of the Assembly elections. He deferred it for the new government to take action. It was a fitting democratic gesture.

The Vizhinjam Project

Vizhinjam Harbour could very well be the biggest natural harbour in Asia. The project's initial expenditure estimates are pegged at 2,500 crores. Kerala has been awaiting its arrival for decades. The project was, in fact, first envisaged during the Maharaja's regime, more than half a century ago.

The previous UDF government had invited an international tender for it. Of the two tenders received then, Zoom Developers alone was qualified for the work. The LDF government that followed also favoured the Zoom tender at first. A great deal of effort was put into getting a central clearance for it. Since a Chinese company was partnering Zoom, the Centre said a firm 'No' to it. When the tenders were re-invited, Zoom, now in partnership with a British firm, offered to do the work for 447 crores. The government favoured Lanco Kondappally who offered to do it for only 115 crores. It could mean a loss of 332 crores to the state exchequer as it was a BOT project. This deal was cancelled by the High Court. The Court asked the government to consider Zoom's bid too, and then opt for the better offer. The government sought to move the Supreme Court in their favour; it proved of no use.

OC fought against the government stand inside and outside the Assembly, and exposed their interests which went contrary to those of the state.

Against the Lottery Mafia

The lottery business has been flourishing in Kerala. The state has been drained of crores of rupees. The loss was not just the exchequers. The poor of the land were being looted in the name of the Sikkim and Bhutan lotteries. They had become addicted to it because of its attractive offers, prizes, draws, advertisements, packages etc. A vigilance report in 2006 found that 22.60 crores worth Sikkim and Bhutan Lotteries were bought by Keralites every day! It was conducted in fraudulent ways and even the prize money was not distributed properly. The CPM has been under fire in this regard. The *Deshabhimani*, the official newspaper of the CPM, had received two crore rupees from the lottery king Santiago Martin as deposit. Kairali TV, the official news channel of the CPM, also received crores of rupees as advertisement for the exclusive live telecast of the draws of Sikkim and Bhutan lotteries; both distributed by Martin. There were also many allegations against the inappropriate manner in which these lotteries were conducted.

OC deputed V. D. Satheeshan to make a direct attack on the government in the Assembly. The LDF government was forced to take action. The *Deshabhimani* repaid the money; Kairali TV stopped the live telecast of lottery draws. The government constituted a high level body of officials to look into the matter. An ordinance was issued to empower the government in this line. As a result, the sale of Sikkim and Bhutan lotteries came to a halt in Kerala. Now the CM has urged the Centre to institute a CBI probe into the lottery scandal here.

The Attapadi Tribal Land

Attappadi, one of the prominent forest regions of Kerala is situated in the northeastern part of the Palghat district of Kerala. It's main inhabitants are the tribals who are exploited all round. Some of the tribals of Attapadi have been fleeced of their land holdings. Private agents have been busy buying up these lands for negligible amounts. Suzlon Company purchased 232 acres of tribal land with the help of forged documents, and put up 33 huge windmills there. OC visited the place for a field study. His frontal assault on the government in this connection forced them to seek a report from the District Collector and the Chief Secretary. Both of them pointed out the massive irregularities committed in the transaction. There ensued a massive hue and cry and the government finally decided to hand over the land to the tribals.

When the Mangroves were Encroached

When the CPM tried to encroach on the mangroves at Pappinissery in Kannur, it posed a threat to the eco-system there. They built a park there and collected fees from the visitors. Environmentalists held protest marches, but were beaten up. OC went to the place and made a detailed study of the situation. The state government paid him no heed. He approached the central government. The environmentalists sought court intervention. Despite strictures from the High Court, the Supreme Court, and the Union Environmental Ministry, the CPM kept playing hide and seek to retain the possession of the Mangroves Theme Park. The mangroves and the rare birds there are, meanwhile, facing extinction.

The Munnar Issue

The land encroachments in Munnar, a hill station in Kerala, came into the limelight when OC visited the region in May 2007. These were largely made by the affiliates of the CPI and CPM, or with their consent and support. Deputy Tahsildar Ravindran had issued title deeds to various Communist leaders, but these deeds were not legally valid. The CPI had got land there in the name of the former CM, P. K. Vasudevan Nair, by depicting him as a landless peasant. The CPM had got it by presenting their District Secretary M. M. Mani as a poor landless farm labourer! Both the parties' illegal buildings are palatial, with luxurious facilities. The CM visited Munnar six times and sent three special squads to clean up the irregularities in Munnar. Some hotels were demolished but others got protection from the court. Encroachments by the CPM leaders and followers were protected by the party. The CM had also declared that 50,000 acres of land, illegally occupied by the Tata's, would also be evicted. But nothing happened. When these things were exposed, the whole eviction affair was evidently doomed to be a fiasco. All the illegal occupants got away scot-free.

The Land Mafia

The CPM had been pretending, for long, to fight against the land mafia operating in the state. But they sold the land of the farm labourers in R Block, Alleppey, to the tourist mafia. In 1972, government under the then CM, C. Achutha Menon, had taken over this land, arduously reclaimed from the lake for cultivation by Joseph Muricken; the same had been distributed among the labourers.

An enquiry was conducted by the party; the report was against the sale. No measures were taken to find the culprits, or to re-distribute the land to their rightful owners. OC pointed out all these details to the CM; his demands remain unheeded to date. Likewise, his timely intervention prevented the Left government from doling out land in Ponmudi. 707 acres of government land had been denotified in such a manner and with unmannerly haste for dubious purposes. OC battled against it both inside the Assembly and out among the public. The government was forced to scrap the scandalous deal.

Tearful Kannur

Kannur has been the sorrow of Kerala for decades. Unfortunately, its tear filled days are not quite over. The National Crime Records Bureau has reported that in 2007, 2008 and 2009, Kerala stood first in the national crime rate, and that Kannur topped the list of towns for riots and violence. In 2007 alone, 16 politically motivated murders were committed in

Kannur. Against this background, OC and the KPCC President Ramesh Chennithala took out peace marches there on 11, 12, and 13 December 2007. From Payyannur to Thalassery, multitudes rallied together behind the duo in this Communist citadel. Quite a sight indeed! OC fasted there on another occasion when the bloodbath continued unabated.

When OC was CM, he had appointed the best police officials in Kannur, and they were given a free hand to contain the violence there. It worked wonders and peace reigned there. Kannur often becomes a centre for bloodbaths when the LDF rules the state, and the police are politically handcuffed.

The Sabarimala Matter

OC reacted sharply in 2007 when the Left government failed to facilitate a safe and smooth ascent for the pilgrims to Sabarimala. The discord in the government and in the Travancore Devaswom Board had reached it's lowest ebb. The result was that the pilgrims were stranded. Conditions have not improved even now. On 14 January 2011, over 100 pilgrims were killed in a stampede near the hill-shrine after the Makarajyothi darshan.

OC does know about the difficulties that the Ayyappa pilgrims have had to face. He always held in reverence the need for Sabarimala development; it had a special place in the state's own progress. Shree Ayyappan's shrine in the wilderness is truly unique. The holy abode stretches across 18 hills, 3,135 ft above the sea level. Annually, crores of pilgrims tread the holy path for spiritual fulfillment. It hurt OC very much when the developmental projects, viz., Sabarimala Master Plan (approximate cost–320 crores) and Pampa Action Plan (approximate cost–356 crores), launched in Sabarimala when he had been the CM, were overthrown.

To Strike against the Centre

The Left government has always tried to harp on the theme of the Centre's neglect of the state. When the rains played havoc in Kerala in 2007, they lodged a complaint; the Chief Minister vowed to fast in front of the Prime Minister's residence. The Central government had, however, received Kerala's application for financial assistance only five days after the declaration of this strike! The LDF then withdrew from their Delhi march.

On another occasion they accused the Centre of curtailing the ration supply to Kerala, and led a protest strike in Delhi. The CM, the ministers, and the MPs joined the demonstration. In fact, the decision did not affect the Below Poverty Line but only the Above Poverty Line and that too because the Centre did not have enough food grains in store. The states with excess produce should have supplied more to the Centre. Bengal was selling their excess food grains to Bangladesh in the black market but no to the Centre; a point the Left government of Kerala had conveniently ignored.

OC has the list of central assistances and packages with him. It amounted to over 50,000 crores. Kerala has witnessed massive investments and assistances from the UPA government. The Government of India established several of its institutions in Kerala, such as Brahmos Aerospace, Hindustan Aeronautics, Unit, Railway Coach Factory Indian, Institute of Space Technology, India Institute of Science Education and Resarch, Defence Ship Building Unit and so on. A. K. Antony, as Defence Minister, was instrumental in bringing to the state quite a few such institutions under his Ministry. The Idukki Package (1,161 crore rupees) and the Kuttanadu Package (1,840 crore rupees) won the hearts and minds of the people there.

A Torn Mask

One of the most tragic sex scandals to rock Kerala, the Kiliroor-Kaviyoor molestation case quickly assumed political colour. If returned to power, he would arrest all the suspects and accomplices in the infamous case; VS had declared as Opposition Leader. Once he assumed the CM's office however, he forgot all about it. Shari, the victim of the Kiliroor case, was sexually abused by several people who lured her into a trap by offering her roles in TV serials. A woman named Latha Nair was the agent. In a related incident, a Namboothiri family in Kaviyoor, who also had a connection with Latha Nair, committed suicide. Their teenage daughter Anagha was also subjected to rape and sexual harassment.

On her fifth death anniversary, Shari's father Surendran, along with his wife and Shari's daughter, tried to hold a *dharna* in front of the official residence of the CM, demanding a reinvestigation of the case. They were chased away by the police. OC introduced the subject in the Assembly by way of a submission. The Left government played evasive on that score.

Surendran now ekes out a meagre livelihood by selling lottery tickets. He has taken a solemn vow not to shave off his beard until the culprits are booked. His beard has begun to touch his belly even as justice recedes steadily. Shari S. Nair had fallen into the clutches of a sex racket at the age of 17. She got pregnant after the traumatic experience and died during the delivery. The previous UDF government had referred Shari's case to the CBI.

The Farmers under a Yoke

Kerala produces only four lakh tons of rice when she annually needs 40 lakh tons of it. The CPM-led union rose against mechanised harvesting in the erstwhile paddy paradise of Kuttanad, and hundreds of acres of paddy fields were laid to waste. The price of rice rose to 25 rupees per kg from 15 rupees, in only two years. OC joined the rank and file of men protesting against the CPM tyranny in Kuttanad.

The farmers there have no right to even try cultivating another crop even when paddy cultivation leads them into a debt trap. When some of them had tried to plant banana and coconut palms, the CPM followers under the leadership of VS came with sickles and axes to cut them down.

The notorious *Vettinirathal* or 'Cut Down Campaign'! Even when he was Chief Minister, the 'Cut Down' continued. OC was dead against this barbaric practice, and inspired the farmers to fight for their l egitimate rights.

The farmers cannot pursue their occupation unless farming proves to be profitable. OC understands this very well. He has his roots in Kumarakom, a hub of paddy-growing families; his mother Baby Chandy hails from there.

The Asian Development Bank Loans

As opposition leader, OC easily exposed the double standards that the CPM took with regard to the ADB loans.

It was in 1997, during the earlier LDF rule, that Kerala first sought loans from the ADB. For a couple of years they pursued the project. The Pokhran Nuclear Tests led to an abrupt ban of all foreign assistance, including the ADB loans. When the UDF came to power in 2001, they resumed the borrowing efforts. The LDF let loose a series of violent strikes to bring the move to naught. When the ADB officials came for negotiations in Kerala, the CPM created unwarranted, unruly disturbances; they even poured oil waste on the heads of the visiting dignitaries.

When the LDF returned to rule, they had no qualms about availing the loans. All that they had propagated against the ADB business was silently washed away in no time. OC unmasked this insincere approach that the CPM and their allies have always taken in matters of this kind.

The Korean Contract

The Restructured Accelerated Power Development and Reform Programme was misused in the state. By awarding the contract to a Korean company, and ignoring the guidelines stipulated, Kerala was likely to forfeit 50 crores. OC pointed out how the state was about to lose a chance to reform the entire power sector. It was suspected that some vested interest was lurking behind this bargain. Later, the CM also expressed his apprehensions and the deal was scrapped.

The Self-financing Institutions

The self-financing institution is at the centre of controversy in Kerala. More than half a crore Keralites are working outside the state and abroad, thanks to their educational qualifications. Imparting quality education through private participation has not been in the CPM grain. The sad plight in Kerala is that the government has little money to improve even the existing educational facilities. The previous UDF government went ahead with self-financing institutions. By 2006, when the UDF government was replaced by the LDF, there were around 25,000 engineering seats and 2,500 medical seats in Kerala. In Tamil Nadu, there are over one lakh engineering seats; and in Karnataka it is well above half a lakh. The plain truth is that most of these seats are occupied by Malayalee students, paying exorbitant fees.

The Left parties have shown their double dealing again in the way they dealt with the self-financing institutions in the state. Thousands of students are studying in this sector. Many of the Left leaders have sent their children to such institutions. Yet the government has offered them nothing but uncertainty. No measures with desirable effect have been taken to date. And now the managements are fleecing their students. As a result Tamil Nadu and other states get plenty of students to fill their seats while many seats in Kerala lie vacant.

In an Hour of Need

When OC was CM, his office was always open to anyone seeking help of any sort. Very many came in there, especially for medical assistance. OC granted such aid for as many as 60,196 people. All within a year and a half!

And then the Left came to power. They refused to hand out any help for the 52,000 applicants whose cases OC had okayed. He was deeply upset and reacted angrily. Slowly, the government relaxed its tough stance and quite a number of applicants benefited by OC's relentless pursuit.

On 12 May 2006, four men met with a tragic end while working in a well. OC requested the government to grant 50,000 rupees each to the four families. The government gave only 10 per cent of it. OC observed the precedent when 50,000 rupees each had been granted. His appeal fell on deaf ears. So he went about collecting funds from his friends and the general public, and handed over 50,000 rupees each to the four families.

The newly introduced single-window admission to the Higher Secondary Course produced the first martyr in Aswathy (17) of Mananthavady. When she did not get admission due to the 'window' bottlenecks, she was unbearably disappointed. OC struck hard at the government's thoughtless ineptitude and heartless indifference in the matter. He asked the government to grant a handsome compensation to Aswathy's family. The Left government gave only a pittance of 30,000 rupees when they had happily given 10 lakh rupees to the family of a CPM criminal killed in Kannur Central Jail.

OC wrote three letters to the Education Minister, M. A. Baby, calling the latter's attention to the callous injustice involved in the Aswathy case. His epistolary efforts were of no use. He took it up as a challenge, and went about raising a relief fund. He then handed over the 2.75 lakhs he had collected to the poor family, in September 2008.

To Strive and Not to Yield

OC's tireless days continue. He would not sit quiet on the laurels of the parliamentary triumph in 2009 or the local administrative bodies sweep in 2010. As a creative Opposition Leader he has to remain prepared against the slings and arrows of outrage that the state's individuals and groups might be inflicted with. He is the saddest to see the many development activities and social security measures, initiated by his government, having failed to take off during the LDF regime.

He has been constantly militating against the government policies, both within the Assembly and outside. A living testament of his speeches in the House is *Janasabdathinu Nalpathandu* (The Voice of the People for 40 Years), officially released by Former President A. P. J. Abdul Kalam on 30 December 2010.

OC is now getting ready for a great leap forward. On 10 January 2011 he started on a 25-day yathra across the state. This odyssey was undertaken in a symbolic bid to end the LDF misrule in Kerala, and to usher in UDF days of progress and plenty.

He takes up every issue that affects the commoner. He will not leave any stone unturned to expose the inefficiency and indifference of the Left government. At the same time, his ready hand reaches out to the needy, everywhere and always. OC often travels the length and breadth of Kerala.

He does not own a car in his home town, Puthupally and hires private taxies occasionally. The taxi drivers find it extremely difficult to cope with his hectic schedules which start from early morning and continue till late at night. In between there might not be a break for food or rest. Most of the taxi drivers are reluctant to oblige him on his trips.

Once OC was in a taxi when the driver got a call on his mobile enquiring whether he was available for a ride in the evening. 'I have a headache with me right now. God alone can say when this will end,' the man replied.

CHAPTER TWO

A 24 X 7 CM

When OC was in office, the Kerala Chief Minister's Chamber was visible via the website. Each and every movement in the room was transmitted, minute by minute, to the world outside by the webcam. The action was seen live through the day. Many objected to this open-door policy. Many people frequent the CM's office and some of them would have liked to keep their visit secret and private. There could be a danger in making public all the visitors and happenings there.

OC however, was striving for transparency in public affairs. His attitude was, 'My office is open to all. None need come here for any shady deal.' The national media gave wide publicity to this bold move. It was for the first time that a CM's office was made so easily accessible to all not only in India but abroad also. The transparent manner in which he had gone about it was remarkable too. Congratulations poured in from far and near.

One of these was from the then President of India, A. P. J. Abdul Kalam. His message read, 'My congratulations on the live telecast of your interactions with the public in the Chief Minister's Office.' The President had seen a crowd in the CM's office, and had taken it for the CM's Mass Contact Programme which had recently been held in the district headquarters of the state, attracting huge crowds. He could hardly guess that it was a telecast of the daily routine in OC's office.

A Dramatic Entrance

When OC assumed office as the 19th Chief Minister of Kerala on 31 August 2004, it marked an unexpected turn of events.

He had played second fiddle in Kerala's Congress politics for quite some time. He was in no hurry for positions and did not sweat in the corridors of power for the same. He, more often than not, gave way to others. That he now was elevated to the premiership of the Ministry seemed an overdue reward for his painstaking past. To date, he has held ministerial office for less than five years in total: Labour Minister for one and a half years in 1977–1978; Home Minister for 80 days in 1981; and Finance Minister for three years from 1991.

OC had placed three conditions if he were to become CM. One, he would not accept the CM chair if A. K. Antony (AK) was to be removed from it. Two, he would not wear the CM's *topi* as part of a package, or on the basis of any compromise. Third and last, if the Party High Command had anybody else in mind, he would not don the CM's robe.

A. K. Antony voluntarily withdrew from the scene. OC's first condition was thus easily met. AK took upon himself the responsibility for the defeat of the UDF in the Lok Sabha elections of 2004, and he resigned on 29 August 2004.

AK met Congress President Sonia Gandhi at the Trivandrum airport on her return from Quilon (She had taken part in the Sree Narayana Guru Jayanti celebrations there) on 29 August 2004. AK discussed his resignation with her and within 10 minutes of her departure for Delhi he made the dramatic declaration of his resignation.

He explained that he had planned to quit soon after the Lok Sabha election debacle, and that he had told Sonia Gandhi about it. For one reason or the other, his withdrawal from office had to be postponed. The uncertainty had gone on for too long. He was now allowed to pull out and so he did.

Ahmed Patel (Political Secretary to Sonia Gandhi) had called OC from Delhi and requested him to meet Sonia Gandhi before she left Kerala. OC also met her at the airport but he did not then oblige the media with any details.

Some of his aides and confidants urged him to ask K. Karunakaran and Vakkom Purushothaman, veteran Congress leaders for help after AK's resignation. He did not do so because he did not want any strings attached to the CM's office if and when it was offered to him. He wished to work without fearing anyone and the shadow of anyone's favour clouding his work.

The party's central observers, Pranab Mukherjee, Margaret Alva, and Ahmed Patel arrived on the scene. The KPCC office-bearers met at Indira Bhavan at nine in the morning on 30 August. Later in the day KPCC President Thennala Balakrishna Pillai and General Secretary Kodikunnel Suresh met Ahmed Patel at the Government Guest House, Thycaud, and passed on to him the decision of the KPCC.

At 3.30 pm, the central leaders held an interview with the Congress MLAs. Each of them was asked, 'Who should be the next CM?' Most of the MLAs proposed OC for the job. Some of the 'I' Group MLAs had advanced Vakkom Purushothaman's name but he withdrew from the race. At 8.30 pm OC was elected unanimously and declared the leader. At 9.30 pm, the UDF met at Cliff House, the official residence of the CM, and announced their support for him; they gave it in writing to Anil Shastri, the party secretary, who handed it over to Governor R. L. Bhatia.

The Support and the Armour

AK described OC's accession as a debt being paid. OC had always stood by him, firmly and faithfully, for four decades. He had taken over from AK on two other occasions earlier, once as president of the KSU and later as the president of the Youth Congress. This was in 1965. AK was Kerala Students Union President and OC, its Secretary. One morning AK came to Kottayam from Ernakulam for a meeting. OC received him and as they were both hungry, they had tea and dosas. When they went to the counter to pay the bill, both realised that neither had any money. AK took up a daily and started reading while OC sat looking up and down the road. He then saw a man from Puthupally pass by and requested him. The man obliged him with the money and the two were finally free to leave.

They indeed walked side by side, for years. On both occasions when AK headed the UDF Ministry, OC stepped aside so that others could find ministerial berths. Whenever the ministry had to face allegations or challenges, OC was always there in the vanguard to defend it. He suavely warded off all the blows from the Opposition, both inside and outside the Assembly.

The Congress Finds a New Team

On 31 August 2004, P. K. Kunhalikutty, K. M. Mani, K. R. Gouriamma, and M. V. Raghavan were sworn in along with OC. It was decided that Kerala Congress (B) and Kerala Congress (Jacob) would be excluded from the UDF Ministry. The Muslim League reconstituted their ministerial fraction. It was never an easy job to select the Congress ministers. Creed, region, and community considerations often held sway over the decision and besides all this, one also had to satisfy the 'Group' demands. The 'I' Group advanced N. Sakthan, Adoor Prakash, and P. P. George.

OC was prepared to accommodate the first and the second. He met with gross disrespect when he called on the Congress stalwart Karunakaran to sort out matters and the two had a falling out. OC made it clear that he would not bow before threat of any kind. Experienced hands and younger ones formed a balanced ministry. All the ministers were sworn in within five days of the CM's assuming of office. At first OC was reluctant to handle the portfolio of Home Affairs.

On the third day after the ministry was formed, the '100-Day Action Drive Programme' was announced. At the next Cabinet meeting, it was decided that Kovalam Palace would be taken over by the government. When the central government had sold the ITDC-owned Asoka Hotel to a private party, the adjacent palace and its 4.21- hectare premises were also handed over to them.

All controversial projects were frozen. The Express Way project was also abandoned. The Express Way is a 507 km long high-speed corridor connecting Trivandrum and Kasargode. It was planned by the A.K. Antony government but the LDF and a section of the media spoke vociferously against it. Kerala has a high density of vehicles and traffic jams are a big problem in major roads and cities. This would have been a solution. Some LDF MLAs later expressed their opinion that it could be beneficial for the state though they had opposed it tooth and nail for three years. Similarly, the Left was against the ADB loans though the city corporations under their control came forward to accept the facility.

A Different Chief Minister

The people have always been OC's strength and weakness alike. So much so that it is said that only when he is lost in a throng that he breathes alright! It did not change even when he became the Chief Minister of Kerala.

The CM's Office and its premises wore a festive air. Visitors were welcome anytime and they could meet their CM without prior appointments and other bureaucratic procedures. As CM, his official meetings, ceremonies, and responsibilities doubled. Nevertheless, he would not turn away from people who sought his assistance.

OC always gave first priority to his visitors, no matter how busy he was or how many important meetings he had to attend to. Many of these people were the commonest of the common man. The sick, the aged, the physically challenged, those who had travelled long distances to see the CM, all found in OC a patient and empathetic listener. The CM would call them all into his office and he would stand amidst them, looking into their complaints and sharing their grievances. If the crowd could not be contained inside his office, he would go out to them, huddled together in the adjacent hall. Whenever he found people awaiting his arrival he would approach them and listen with a patient ear before he resumed his official routine.

Multitudes would turn up to meet him. Most of them came with complex problems and he was very often their last resort. They would, at times, behave in unpredictable ways. Some even prostrated before him. Aghast, he would jump backwards. Some even embraced him out of deep gratitude and affection. Sometimes these meetings also offered occassion for fun and laughter.

Once a visitor walked up to him and declared, 'Sir, I have some good news for you.'

'What's it?'

'I've developed a remedy for AIDS, sir.'

'That's fine indeed.'

'I need somebody to try it upon, sir!'

The CM was startled. As usual he passed on the onerous responsibility to his APS. He asked the man to proceed to the MLA Hostel; he was sure to find a guinea-pig there.

The man persisted.

'What else can I do for you?' demanded the CM.

'Please, sir, spare me the auto fare to reach there.'

The man managed to collect 100 rupees from his CM!

When the Congress candidate was defeated in the Trivandrum Lok Sabha by-elections in 2005, there were strong rumours that OC would resign from office. That evening he faced the media. This reinforced the rumour and a big crowd collected around his office. After the press conference, the CM came out to collect complaints and memorandums from the pressing people. One of those assembled there, handed him a blank sheet of paper.

'There's nothing written on it,' observed the CM.

'You need to only sign on it, sir. I'll enter the matter later,' replied the complacent the complainant.

The district-wise sessions of the Mass Contact Programme introduced by the CM fetched 96,901 complaints in all. Of these, 42,151 ones were settled immediately. Within a year of his assuming office as CM, OC received 2,03,200 complaints. Some of these were mailed directly to him while others poured in via the CM's website, Transparent Kerala Call Centre, and the CM's Grievance Cell.

Wherever he went, there would be bundle of appeals and complaints awaiting him. He would take them back to Trivandrum where they would be listed and catalogued, and placed before the CM for his signature. Merely signing them alone could be physically taxing. Each time the CM came back after a journey, two or three boxfuls of these were sure to accompany him. He used to spend all his spare time perusing and signing them, for further action. Whenever he received a call, he would take it with his left hand while his right continued signing away.

Once, the CM was to hold discussions with 'cultural' leaders on 'Vision 2010' at the Thycaud Guest House at 9.30 in the morning. OC reached there on time but except for a few, the 'cultural' leaders had not turned up. He talked to those present for a while and then signalled his gunman to get him some of the 'complaints' from his car. He then set himself to his signing task. The 'cultural' leaders, who arrived late, were spared the embarrassment. They had not wasted the CM's time after all.

Crowds and complaints were nothing new to OC. He had reached the heights of decision-making in Kerala politics without the backing of loud mouthed philosophy, crowd-pulling rhetoric, or any incomparable organisational skills. He had one indispensable plus point: he never severed his umbilical cord from the people at large. That is, he had forged for himself a political culture by bringing together a mosaic of personal relations in public life.

OC would be rather ill at ease if he did not come across a few complaints a day. He wanted to see pleas and petitions every day. He was also keen to solve in the least a few problems every day, or else the day was as good as lost for him.

One of the famous men of letters, George Onakkoor, was witness to a curious incident. He called on OC once when the latter was out of power at his Puthupally House in Jagathy in Trivandrum. There were only a few visitors there that day. Onakkoor saw two children with some papers in their outstretched hands. OC accepted those papers with a smiling headshake. His wife Mariamma explained to Onakkoor that their children had thus teasingly found an easy way to keep their petition-hungry father fed.

OC has a way with the crowds. He resorts to certain shortcuts to manage them. Usually, he collects their complaints, one by one; scribbles the necessary suggestions on these, and hands over the same to the officers standing by him. Rarely does he call a complainant apart and speak in private to him/her. He might place his hand on the person's shoulder if the petitioner happened to be someone close to him. If a phone call could clinch the matter, he would call the concerned person instantly and have them deal with the case.

Complaints and petitions were entered in the minutes, and placed before the CM. When he had signed them, they would be dispatched to the respective departments. This was the established routine. Each petitioner would be informed by the CM's office the details regarding the number and date of the paper received, and the officer concerned who would go into the substance of the case.

The CM's office is usually under stringent supervision and visitors are strictly regulated. But this was not the case during OC's term there. Usually, visitors' time is restricted from 3 to 5 pm. This schedule was done away with and the security personnel had a tough time. They once had a nerve-wracking hour when the DYFI followers pushed into the Secretariat demanding the resignation of Health Minister K. K. Ramachandran Master. The protestors managed to reach the second floor of the building, to the CM's office, raising pandemonium.

The daunting number of the visitors never bothered OC; none of them were sent back disappointed. The CM would hear them out, every single one of them and attend to all their appeals. Though it was, of course, impossible for every complaint to be settled and every problem solved.

OC is blessed with an extraordinary memory. He can grasp things fast and easily. He can recall whom he had met before, and name them, to their astonishment. Whenever he presided over a conference, he would steer the discussions clear of running aground in needless digression. He was always ready with timely suggestions and he had the knack for arriving at quick solutions. High-level conferences would not last more than half an hour. Even at the Party Executive meetings, OC would not spend more time than it was really necessary. He only needed to be informed of the decisions taken and he would take care of the rest.

On a Continuous Journey

In addition to crowds and complaints, OC is eager to go on journeys. His life seems to be all about trips and travel. A journey without end! One can safely say that there is no other politician traveller like him. Once M. M. Hassan, the Congress Party spokesman, observed about OC's continual journeys, 'Nobody knows when he started these journeys; nobody knows when he would stop to rest.' Hassan had adapted a famous verse from a Malayalam film lyric to add flavour to his comment.

OC began his travels when he was the president of the KSU. As CM, the miles he travelled did not just double but also trebled. Within a year in office, the state-given Ambassador carried him over 47,000 kms with more miles added by air and rail. One special facet of his travels is that he finds time to make up for his lost nocturnal slumber during these. Another gain was that he could sign those complaints and requests assigned to the CM's Office. While on the move he could also have long telephone conversations which were nearly impossible when he was in the CM's chamber.

A speeding vehicle was ideal for his sleep. With his head bent forward and sitting by the left door of his car, OC would regain his lost sessions of nightly sleep. After stepping into the CM's Office he had to confront many a day of conflict. He would, on all these occasions, remain as cool as cool could be.

After the split in the Congress in Kerala, OC, as CM, had to face the Assembly by-elections at Azheekode and Koothuparambu in Kannur, in 2005. Both were the CPM's incumbent seats. Calculations were afoot that the CPM lead would dwindle at Koothuparambu, and the Congress could get a slender chance at Azheekode. Contrary to all expectations, the CPM came out in flying colours from both the constituencies. When the counting was in progress, OC was on his way from Kottayam to Trivandrum. He tracked the trends which were adverse and then he slipped quietly and calmly into his customary nap. What could not be mended could be ended by a soothing forty winks!

No special preparations were made even for his long journeys. One or two pairs of clothing with a few other necessities were sufficient for him. The CM boarding a flight with a small brief case in hand was a familiar sight those days. His Delhi flights were always at night; this was to save his office time. He would arrive from Delhi at dawn, and be at the CM's Office at eight in the morning. Many a morning has witnessed this OC practice.

One ominous Tuesday, the CM and several Ministers had accompanied the corpse of Central Minister P. M. Sayyid to Lakshadweep. The weather was unfavourable for them to make the return journey the same day. It was a bit late when the party took off for Trivandrum the following morning which was a Wednesday. At 9 am every Wednesday morning, there would be a cabinet meeting. OC arrived at the airport only at 10.30 am. He headed straight for the meeting while a change of clothes were sent from home. Unfortunately, the shirt that was sent had no buttons. Pins replaced the buttons for the day and the CM hurried on to the conference without even a bite of breakfast. After that there was a heavy schedule to attend to. It was in the evening, when he boarded the flight to Delhi, that he had his first meal of the day!

There were only two CMs in India who would fly economy class: A. K. Antony and Oommen Chandy. At the Congress CMs' conference in Chandigarh, Sonia Gandhi emphasised the necessity of leading a simple life. The CMs of other states travel to Delhi with a large retinue. OC would often make his Delhi trips almost always alone.

He would not bother about discomforts wherever he went. His credo is that what has to be done has to be done and that too as quickly as possible, personal inconvenience notwithstanding. This has always been the motivating force behind the OC line of action.

Of the many incidents that illustrate his credo, here is one. Once when OC was UDF Convener, he was to travel by the Second Class AC coach of Kannur Express to Trivandrum. There was some confusion about his reservation but he was told that the TTE would settle it on the train. The train arrived at Kottayam station at two in the morning and OC boarded it. OC did not feel like waking anyone or switching on the lights. He stood in the narrow space outside the bays of the compartment. He had had a grilling schedule. Now he was spent and sleep was getting the best of him. He could not keep standing any longer. So he sat down on the floor by the door, trying in vain to keep sleep at bay. He had to leap to his feet whenever the train stopped at a station lest the passengers should see the UDF Convener asleep, squatting on the floor of the train. This three squatting-standing cycle continued until the train reached Kazhakkuttam near Trivandrum around five in the morning and the TTE spotted him to his thankful relief.

OC does not wear a watch though he travels so widely and so often, and attends so many meetings and conferences. Yet he is on time everywhere, and for everything. Very rarely does he turn up late. It certainly is no small wonder that OC can be punctual despite his unadorned wrist. Delay has not seriously impaired his programmes, either. His biological clock is unerringly accurate and it enables him to sleep (perchance to dream!) or to wake up, as occasion demands. OC had had a watch in his youth. He would frequently lose it and so he decided to do without it, entirely. A. K. Antony is his guru in this regard. OC's life's seconds number themselves without hindrance; they keep him going faithfully, punctually.

Camel's Food

As a busy CM, the first thing he sacrificed was his meals. After meeting people at his home in the morning, if there was no time for breakfast he would skip the same, and set out on his day's odyssey. His lunch would be brought to his office. It was not certain when he might have a morsel of it, though.

The visitors must have departed before he would sit down to food. They would hardly ever leave him alone. Too often, the lunch (brunch, at times) would serve as supper. According to K. A. Chandran, MLA, OC eats a stomachful when he gets it and then he can survive for long without a bite. Quite like the camel!

He is star-crossed as far as food is concerned, explains OC. He was born under the *anizham* star, and is fated to wander without proper food and rest. As a wedding-guest, his record might remain unbroken! He has hardly ever stopped for a nuptial feast. Only on a few occasions has he enjoyed a taste of the same. Naturally, the people concerned would be too close to him to bid him an earlier goodbye sans the repast.

Once he sat down for such a feast. A plantain leaf was placed before him but then came the rub! They could not find the bride's *thali* (mangalsutra) anywhere. The guests and hosts joined the search. OC's time was running out fast. He could not wait any longer as he had an urgent mission to embark on. He bade the party adieu without a mouthful. On another occasion, the food was served and the feast started. A similar problem cropped up. One among the bride's party could not find her gold chain anywhere. Everyone gathered there had to be searched; it led to a squabble. OC left the place, unnoticed, unfed.

These incidents had occurred before he was CM of the state. As CM, things did not improve, gastronomically speaking. One afternoon, he started from Trivandrum by the Chennai Mail. It was 3 p m. His gunman gave him a masala dosa, his first meal of the day. However, when his gunman opened the small polythene bag for the sambar, it spilt the savoury contents onto his shirt. Since he did not have a change of clothes, he took off his shirt and washed it clean himself. In the meanwhile he lost his appetite for the food.

The masala dosa has always been a gourmet's choice for him since his student days. At hotels where he is a regular, he does not have to place the orders; they serve him the masala dosa and its accompaniments. He likes it best with chilled soda. Fellow-student and friend, K. C. Joseph, MLA has also fallen for this food habit after years of acquaintance with OC. The chilled soda is a godsend for those with little money and little time to have anything really solid for it slows down the pangs of hunger!

One day, OC was extremely busy tending to his duties that he had no time for food. He reached the city airport at four in the evening for his flight to Delhi. There was a 10 minute delay for the take-off. His APS urged him to have some sustenance. OC washed his hands and sat down at the table in the VIP lounge. Some attendants went to his car to get the grub. There was no trace of it there. His driver had sent it back home. He had thought that the CM had already boarded the plane. OC got the wind of it. Without a word of complaint, he wiped his hands, and proceeded to check in for the flight.

Oh, the Speed!

The UDF government had less than two years left when OC assumed the CM's office. The new government longed for a new slogan. They hit upon 'Kerala Fast Forward'. OC could not have deserved a better slogan. Speed is part of his DNA. From food to decisions, everything is taken with the utmost speed possible. In fact, his quick decision- making has been instrumental in leading him to political heights. His governance too had this same OC speed. As CM, he had an endless procession of programmes to attend. The One Hundred-Day Programme, One-Year Programme, 10+3 Programmes associated with Vision 2010, Nine-Point Programme declared on Independence Day (2005), and so on and so forth.

He says, 'I take decisions very fast. If a hundred issues crop up before me, I should like to take decisions on all hundred of them. It's quite likely that 10 of them go wrong. If wrong I'll correct myself. I am not stubborn or incorrigible.'

At Davos and Back

OC slipped in Davos in Switzerland. It was not in his decisions or in its execution. His speed on the snow made him the slip and he fell down. He was there for taking part in the World Economic Forum on 27 January 2006. Heads of states, heads of large companies, economic experts, and others come to Davos every January to be at the Forum. Central Ministers P. Chidambaram and Kamal Nath, Planning Commission Deputy Chairman Montek Singh Ahluwalia, Delhi Chief Minister Sheila Dikshit, Rajasthan Chief Minister Vasundhara Raje, Reliance Chairman Mukesh Ambani, ITC Chairman Y. C. Deveshwar, and Infosys President Nandan Nilekani were also present there.

OC had planned to present papers on three topics. At the first session he spoke on 'Development Aims for India'. Kerala had to solve the second generation problems arising in the wake of development. Infrastructure had to be bettered for the same. This called for large-scale investment by public and private sectors. OC appealed to the international community to come and invest in the state. OC could not present the other two papers due to his mishap. While the other CMs were accompanied by a large retinue, Principal Secretary Dinesh Sharma IAS alone accompanied OC.

It was bitterly cold in Davos and OC was impatient at wasting a couple of minutes waiting for the car to arrive to pick him up after the first session. He was walking fast to the car when he fell and broke his hip. He had not worn the special shoes for walking on ice. He had instead worn ordinary ones and his customary shirt and dhoti.

OC's wife Mariamma was informed of the accident at four in the morning. She was told that it was not serious. 'Happy company for Amma,' was her first comment. OC's mother Baby Chandy also had a hip problem and had been admitted to the Medical College Hospital, Trivandrum. On the second evening after his return to Kerala, he visited his mother at the hospital despite the doctors' strong restrictions regarding his mobility.

On the seventh day after the accident, OC came back from Switzerland. Two vehicles awaited him at the airport. One was the CM's car; its front seat was laid out with cushions as if it were an ambulance. OC would not get in there. He got into the other car leaning on a walking stick. The crowd and the media surrounded the vehicle. Finance Minister Vakkom Purushothaman (who had the charge of CM in OC's absence), DGP Ramon Srivastava, and others tried in vain to contain the crowd. The car could not move an inch. Everyone was eager to see their CM. OC finally stood up on one foot in the car, and greeted the people. It was only then that they thawed, and made way for him.

On the 17th day, he was back in his office. The lift at the back of the Secretariat took him to the second floor of the building. He moved through the corridor with the help of a walker for about 40 meters. For the first time in his life, this man of speed had to slow down his steps. It was a painful sight indeed.

Office Time at 2 am

OC never cut short CM's office work to pursue the politician's path of public service. On the other hand, he found time by working overtime. His office hours often extended to 2 am! It would be around 11 p m when he saw off the last of his visitors and then he would settle down to his official work, especially the perusal of files. There were 20 departments, including the Home Affairs, under him. OC would usually stand when he went through the files lest he fall asleep in his chair. PS, APS, and others would be his companions on night duty. OC was particular that no file should be kept pending at his office. To expedite this file business, his secretaries would join him on his journeys often.

At times, OC would spend nearly 18 hours a day at the CM's office without a moment's rest or wink of sleep. He would nod off at meetings but he would fight wearily against sleep trying to keep his drowsy eyelids open.

Around 2 am, the CM would leave the office. The security staff, who bade him 'Good Morning' on his arrival, would now bid him 'Good Morning' again at his departure. The Secretariat, the city, and the state at large, would be fast asleep when the CM was on his way home to bed. He would be too hungry and sleepy, to note the sublunary splendour of the secretariat buildings. Besides, he has paid little attention to the daily concerns of everyday life: food, health, clothes, hairstyle, and personal appearance.

Time has indeed been kind to him. Now in his late sixties, OC is quite healthy for his age. No serious ailment has afflicted him so far. All through his years of travel he has met with but a couple of accidents, like the icy fall in Switzerland.

Some Enslaving Habits

Long-accustomed ways went along with him even after OC entered the CM's office. One of them had to do with his hairstyle. Rarely did he go to the barber's. Fashions may come and go but his sideburns have remained the same, running down nearly to the chin though not quite of late. His unruly hair is cut roughly here and there; it refuses to be smoothed down, entirely. When he shaves, the anarchic bristles rear their heads in rebellion against the hasty razor. After his bath he combs once and this suffices for the whole day. The hair keeps getting more and more dishevelled as the day wears on. He does not seem to bother about it. When he appears before the media, or attends a public meeting, he does not spruce up for the show and he applies absolutely no make-up at all.

If it was late when he reached home, he was very particular not to disturb anybody there. He served himself at table and entered his bedroom without turning on the lights. His wife had no idea of this timetable, of when he would come and go. The beauty was that he had only to get into bed and gentle sleep caressed him readily, knitting up his day's ravelled sleeve of care.

After hardly four hours of sleep, OC woke up at 6 or 6.30 in the morning. He started his day with a small prayer and a glance through the newspapers. Some of his files would be waiting for him there. There could be two phones ringing in his ears but the CM himself would answer them.

The crowds would begin to collect in the courtyard quite early in the morning. OC would talk to them. If time permitted, he would treat himself to breakfast. He would leave for the CM's office at 8 am and to the busy schedule of the day as usual.

In power or out of it, OC has always been busy, always amongst the people, ready to shoulder their burden. Busy, without enough rest or respite but intriguing ideas criss-cross his mind all along. Apparently inexhaustible seem his energies, working nearly all day long, and seven days a week! His life is, as it were, an open door; anyone and everyone would find welcome in there, almost always.

Journalist P. C. Sukumaran Nair once wrote, 'If one speaks of a politician who leads a simple life, who is of a calm disposition, kind and gentle to the core; such epithets would not be too many, nor too much, when the same were applied to Oommen Chandy. These would not be base exercises in sycophancy, either. He deserves these, and more. I'd not hesitate to add that he is a man of dignity, and a politician with principles.'

The Development Mantra

All the dailies of Kerala made an assessment of the OC Government when it completed a year in office on 31 August 2005. The *Malayala Manorama* asked 10 people to rate the government and to award marks for its performance. The *Mathrubhumi* set 20 people to identify the government's three most important merits, and an equal number of demerits.

The former Rubber Board Chairman P. C. Syriac awarded OC eight marks out of 10. But the lowest, zero, was given by G. Balamohan Thampi, former VC, Kerala University, and a known Leftist. The average secured OC a First Class.

He had to confront all sorts of problems during his tenure as CM. He obviously worked hard, took quick decisions, and adopted suitable political strategies, to pass for a First Class CM. He travelled far and wide, and established direct contact with the people in a bid to solve their problems. He had a number of remedies for the maladies of the state. He gave the lead to many development activities in Kerala. He would hold several high-level meetings almost daily. The ideas issuing forth from these deliberations, would find immediate execution. Five days of the week OC would be in the state capital; one day would be spent in any one of the districts and Sunday would be reserved for Puthupally, his constituency. This was his set routine.

OC's span in the CM's office, can be divided into three periods. It began with his forging ahead on the wings of interaction with the people. In the second, he made great strides through several development projects. The third phase gave greater emphasis to his popular programmes.

The OC Model

The state's development was OC's first and foremost priority. Everyone the world over now knows that the 'Kerala Model Development' gives importance to social welfare measures. In education, health, and a few other spheres, Kerala's record matched the developed world's and had attracted international attention. The 'Kerala Model' was under stress due to paucity of public funds and private investment.

An Indian-American industrialist, and a member of the Texas Sugar Land City Council, Thomas Abraham observes, 'I'd like to start some business in Kerala. But there is no security guaranteed. Neither the state government nor the community is bothered about it. If conscious efforts are taken to guarantee security to business ventures in Kerala, there are enough and more American Malayalees to turn the state into a demi-paradise.' (*India Today*, 8 Feb. 2006)

The truth is that Kerala is blessed with numerous favourable factors, not to be found in other states like natural beauty, salubrious climate throughout the year, an educated community, electricity, water, enterprising people, and hard-working labourers. 'God's Own Country' has sold tourism to the whole world. The state should be an Eden for investors from across the world. OC, as CM, attempted to create the best possible investment-friendly environment as well as infrastructure development in Kerala.

Cochin: Tomorrow's Singapore

The UDF government's most significant achievement is that it could persuade the Central government to invest 20,000 crores in Kerala.

This naturally ended the decade-old battle-cry that the Centre had been ignoring the state. Cochin, 'The Queen of the Arabian Sea', is all set to gain unprecedented regal heights. It is already the one place that has scored the highest growth rate in the country. The *Sagar Mala* (The Ocean Chain) has been planned for the integral development of Cochin. It includes the Vallarpadam Container Terminal, Petronite LNG Terminal, and other giant projects. Cochin Harbour is going international. Cochin could be tomorrow's Singapore.

Three decades of anxious waiting finally ended in February 2005 when Prime Minister Manmohan Singh laid the foundation stone for the Vallarpadam Container Terminal. 'This new terminal would turn out to be gateway to the world,' observed the Prime Minister. It was completed in 2011, a year and half behind schedule.

Vision 2010

'Vision 2010' was born without any prolonged birth pangs, delivered, as it were, on a lift in the Secretariat. OC signed necessary paper for its implementation as he came down the lift.

On 28 July 2005, President A. P. J. Abdul Kalam shared his 'Vision for Kerala' in the Assembly. It carried 10 planks. The President held a power-point presentation that recognised the strength and weakness of the state. He then engaged a class for the MLAs. He had taught thus in other parts of the country. Nowhere else could he witness such a quick response as he did here.

It was 11am when the President presented his 'Vision' in the AssemblyHe went on with his programme for the day. OC accompanied him. En route the CM made a phone call for a meeting in the evening to discuss the President's proposal; it was to be attended by the members of the Planning Board, and the Secretaries. They met in the CM's chamber at five in the evening for half an hour and they decided to implement Vision 2010. OC was in the lift when he signed the paper for it. He then joined the President on his flight to Cochin. On the following day, in the august presence of the President, OC declared that Kerala was going to implement his Vision. They were together at the reception held in honour of the President at the Rubber Board Office in Kottayam. President Kalam was surprised at OC's rocket speed.

Discussions followed on the floor of the assembly and elsewhere. Three more planks were added to the President's 10-point programme and five task forces were formed. Vision 2010 was to carry out projects worth 13,459 crore rupees. The state government's share would be 16 per cent, the Central government's 6 per cent and the rest would come from private entrepreneurs and financing agencies Poverty eradication, doubling of individual income, reduction of unemployment, trebling of higher education opportunities, facilitating clean and responsible governance, were among its key targets.

The government made large scale preparations and spearheaded two projects. The first was for extracting *neera* from coconut trees, and the other for producing bio fuel from tapioca. But then the Assembly elections were declared and the ventures were destined to be thrown overboard.

Infrastructure Development

Kerala can make rapid progress in infrastructure development when the following were achieved; the development of Trivandrum and Calicut airports, Kannur airport, Kerala's own airways, Cochin Metro, Smart City in Cochin, and the Vizhinjam harbour project. OC realised that the industry best suited for Kerala was the IT sector. Kerala could not provide land for large-scale industries. The Smart City project topped OC's priority list in the IT sector. Once it was realised, Cochin could be India's IT hub. Many other IT firms would follow. Smart City alone could provide one lakh jobs.

The Techno Park at Kariavattom, Trivandrum, was started in 1990. It was the first IT venture in the whole country. Since then other states have gone far ahead but Kerala, the pioneer in a way, has yet to develop this booming sector.

A Special Concern for Sabarimala

Sabarimala is one of the biggest pilgrimage centres of the world. Annually, millions of pilgrims arrive there but the lack of amenities plays havoc every year. OC went up the holy abode of Shree Ayyappan (the *Sannidhanam*) on 24 January 2005. It took only an hour and 10 minutes for him to climb the Neelimala from the Pampa river base. Usually people take about two hours for this rough tread. The CM did not halt anywhere on his way up. Ministers Thiruvanchoor Radhakrishnan, K. C. Venugopal and Adoor Prakash, and the accompanying officials found it difficult to keep pace with him. OC made the trek to appraise the pilgrims' facilities available there. He visited Malikappuram as well.

That was his second visit to Sabarimala. He had earlier visited the holy shrine as a member of a Legislative Committee. It was clear to OC that more forest areas had to be allotted for the Sabarimala Development Project. When he first attended the CMs' meeting which the Prime Minister had convened, the first topic that OC put forward was this very same Sabarimala issue. The PM and his Principal Secretary T. K. A. Nair took active interest in the project. The same was again discussed when the PM came to Kerala to inaugurate the Vallarpadam Container Project and the Centre cleared 12.67 hectares of forest land from the Periyar Tiger Reserve area for the development of Sabarimala.

Central government also sanctioned 356 crores to clean up the Pampa river. The pilgrims begin their journey to the shrine after a dip in this holy river. The UDF government initiated a master plan for Sabarimala which included a queue complex, ropeway, trekking route, etc., for 320 crores.

A Smart Chief Minister

Bringing investments to Kerala and creating an investment-friendly climate for the same, formed OC's focal point of development. He tried to rid the state of bundhs and hartals. Investment slowly began to trickle into both the sectors. The World Bank, the Chamber of Indian Industries, National Productivity Council, NASCOM, and other agencies rated Kerala as having turned quite investment friendly.

Time alone would judge what OC did for Kerala in a year and three quarters. One thing is certain. He projected development as Kerala's main agenda. He snubbed the CPM for having been 'Enemies to Development'. He had not missed the point. For Kerala was soon to witness the changing ways of the CPM in the state. They held a seminar on 'Kerala 2015'. Party Secretary Pinarayi Vijayan led a Kerala march with the motto 'Social Justice and Integral Development'. Even the common man started talking about development.

Probably, this is the reason why noted cultural activist Soorya Krishna Murthy observed that OC was the smartest CM Kerala has so far produced.

A Loving Regard

OC knew well that he had to return to the people, again and again, if he were to give shape to a government of the people, by the people, and for the people. He launched many multi-pronged programmes to win over their confidence, such as the Mass Contact Programme, *Ashraya* Scheme, Health Insurance Scheme, free rations, and rice at three rupees a kg, and so on. He cared for the poor and the needy and that concern came directly from his heart.

The Mass Contact Programme

At each of the 14 district headquarters, from 10 in the morning till midnight, and without a break, their CM patiently heard out the people's pleas and complaints, and shared their anxieties and worries. OC as usual forgot all about his food, for hours on end.

The people who would not dare to enter a village office, those who had wasted years in government offices running from pillar to post, all of them flocked together before their Chief Minister who went to them to hear their pleas. Most of their problems should have been solved long back. They had been brow-beaten and sidelined by overbearing officials who would often go by the letter of the rule, and quote all sorts of rubrics and regulations to defend their inhuman inaction.

In the beginning, the Mass Contact sessions started at 10 in the morning and concluded at six in the evening. It slowly extended to midnight and in Calicut, it went way past midnight. There were well over 10,000 complaints there. OC sat through them all. He could solve problems by the thousands. His kindness and gentleness stood him in good stead. The people and their petitions inspired him to further goodness and tenderness.

A new kind of leader was emerging in Kerala with the success of the One Hundred Day Programme and the Mass Contact Programme. He brought in a new style of functioning and initiated speedy redress of grievances and fast tracking of decisions.

The *Ashraya* Project

Towards the end of her life, old Gracie had suffered cruel days of trepidation in a small hovel at Kuttichal, Nedumangadu. It was particularly horrifying because she had to house her teenage granddaughter Shalini. The place was close to the forest area. There were wild animals on one side and men who had lost their moral reason, on the other. Little wonder, Gracie had turned into a bundle of sagging nerves.

Twelve years back, her unmarried daughter had passed away at childbirth. The child's father was not known. The grandmother had to take care of the little one and as Shalini grew, Gracie's sleepless nights also increased. Kudumbasree's (Kudumbasree is a women oriented, community-based poverty eradiction programme of the Kerala Government) *Ashraya* Project came to her help. They built a house for her. OC handed over the key to the old woman on Deepavali day, 11 November 2004. The Village Panchayat adopted Shalini and met her school expenses. A sense of security began to shed light on this lonely, forlorn pair. OC also visited some of the other 95 poverty stricken families that the *Ashraya* had planned to build houses for. These marginalised people could hardly believe their eyes that their CM had called on them in their tumble-down dwellings.

Ashraya became OC's pet project. Almost all the beneficiaries of the scheme were the unwanted of society: the aged, the mentally retarded, the physically challenged, and the terminally ill. They were taken care of by the Panchayat and the Kudumbasree. In less than two years, OC implemented the *Ashraya* Project in 596 panchayats.

There were 33 lakh women associated with the Kudumbasree; they conducted one and three-quarter lakhs of 'Neighbourhood Gatherings' (*Ayalkoottam*). Many an impoverished family found a living there for their subsistence. The women had hit upon a way to enter the mainstream of public life. OC raised the tone and tenor of this movement.

The Welfare Pension and Medical Aid

OC, as CM, took two proud social security measures. One was to distribute unemployment wages, farm labourers' pension, and other welfare pensions on the first of every month. It meant a monthly amount of 18 crores distributed among 15 lakh people, though each one got only a nominal amount. Yet, it was a sum that gave them a small measure of relief in eventide of their rather neglected life. OC declared in the assembly that he would not draw CM's salary until the monthly welfare pensions were distributed.

The other measure was to give medical aid liberally to as many as possible. The CM could directly grant as much as 5,000 rupees to a deserving person. If recommended by a district collector, it could be raised to the maximum of 10,000 rupees. In a year and a quarter, 13.59 crores was handed out to 60,196 patients who were its beneficiaries.

This timely service became a bitter pill for the CM when he was accused of having diverted the Tsunami Funds for the above purpose. OC reacted sharply to the accusation at a meeting convened for a clarification. He was doubly furious because he had okayed the recommendations put forward by the Opposition MLAs for such medical support and they were now accusing him falsely. Thenceforth, all endorsements were to be thoroughly scrutinised before assistance was granted and only after the necessary ratification by district collectors.

When people sought medical relief through ads in newspapers, the relevant information was collected by the Information and Public Relations Office, and a grant was given. However, no publicity was given to this humanitarian service.

The Narendran Commission Report

The Narendran Commission was an inquiry commission appointed by the Kerala Government in February 2000 to study and reprot on the adequacy or other wise of representation for Backward Calsses in the Public Services of the State.

Amidst many apprehensions, OC decided to implement the recommendations of the Narendran Commission Report early in 2006. Many had warned him against all sorts of communal conflicts and polarisations. An amicable settlement had been arrived at after necessary consultations and negotiations; every section of the community was to be treated justly.

The following were its significant decisions.

1. The reservation percentage meant for every section of the backward classes, should assuredly be theirs.

2. If one of these sections could not present their candidates, the said seats would not be made available for the next community, nor would these be allotted to the general merit quota. Instead these could be left vacant.

3. Direct recruitment could be conducted for these unfilled vacancies.
4. A committee would be set up to supervise the enforcement of reservation; the CM was to chair it. All leading communities welcomed these decisions.

Arundhati's Letter

Another initiative was to give an egg a week to each weak schoolchild, from standards one through seven. This was in addition to the existing noon-meal scheme. The project was very well implemented. But Arundhati Raj, a UKG pupil of Government LP School, Nedumangad, wrote to the CM that the KG kids were left out from the programme while their immediate seniors were cared for. The CM immediately contacted the officials concerned. He ordered eggs to be distributed among nursery and special school pupils as well, it was decided. 53,000 UKG children benefited because of little Arundhati's letter. The Egg Project required 19 crore rupees per annum though.

The CM inaugurated the scheme by handing over an egg to little Arundhati herself and she was the guest on Indiavision's News Hour that day.

One Kilo of Rice for Three Rupees

A grand humanitarian step was taken when it was resolved that the families below the poverty line would be supplied with 25 kg rice a month at three rupees a kg. When the LDF government came to power in 2006, they abandoned this scheme. On the eve of the Lok Sabha elections in 2009, they reintroduced it.

Santhosh in State Car One

Santhosh of O S Bhavan (Edavakkadu, Sreekaryam, Trivandrum) had fallen into the trough of despondence due to blindness, illness, and unemployment. He felt that all would be well if only he could meet the CM. He was taken to the CM's office at the Secretariat several times but OC was on tour in the districts for the Mass Contact Programme, on all those occasions.

The Santhosh story appeared in one of the newspapers. The man thought that the CM might have noticed it. He went to Puthupally House at Jagathy. He stood apart from the crowds there. OC spotted him as he hurried into his official car. He allowed Santhosh to get in and sit beside him and then took him to the CM's office. There was hardly anyone there to see this spectacle of Santhosh stepping out of the CM's car in grand style! It was only eight in the morning.

By birth Santhosh had been blind. He had been making a mediocre living by selling lottery tickets. He had married, but his wife died when she was six months pregnant. He was stricken with kidney disorder and he was too ill to even walk. He could not move around selling the tickets anymore. Santhosh had passed the Telephone Operating Course with First Class. He wanted to start a telephone booth, and had approached the Corporation authorities. He drew a blank. At the end of his car ride with the CM, Santhosh returned home with a grant of 10,000 rupees to start a booth.

Lillykutty's Plea

It was during the CM's Mass Contact Programme at Kottayam that Lillykutty caught public attention. She touched the CM's chin as she narrated her woeful tale. The scene was photographed and later splashed all over the media. This photo was later used by the Information and Public Relations Department as the official photo of the government's 'Transparent Kerala' programme. The people could go so close to their CM as to touch his chin when they went to unburden themselves to him. The message of the picture was too transparent to fail.

Lillykutty came from Veeralasseril House in Changanacherry. She was working as a casual sweeper with the Department of Agriculture. When the CM turned up at Kottayam, she petitioned him to appoint her full-time. He received her application, and ordered for immediate action. But the ruling was that there were many casual sweepers with the Department; to appoint only one of them to a permanent post, could be an act of nepotism. So the Cabinet meeting of 13 July 2005, included Lillykutty on the agenda, and decided to appoint the woman as a full-time sweeper with the Civil Supplies Corporation. That was a welcome alternative.

But Lillykutty did not report for duty. She had her reasons to be fearful for she had only two more years to retire. The change of department might deprive her of her due retirement benefits.

A Motorised Tricycle

As he was physically challenged, Sasikumar(32) of Kochuputhazhathu House (Kudavachur, Vaikom) could not travel very fast. Yet he did travel as fast as he could, and went riding all the way from Vaikom to the CM's office, on his tricycle, covering distance of around 175 kms. He had earlier appeared before the CM at Kottayam when the latter had been there on his Mass Contact Programme. His petition was that his tricycle should be motorised, and that he should be enabled to start selling lottery tickets for a living. The Social Welfare Department had informed him that his application had to be turned down and hence, he undertook this trip to Trivandrum.

Sasikumar earned the necessary money for the journey to the capital by dancing in the streets on his severely disabled legs. It took him a week, braving the drafts of rain, and the sweltering sun, to reach the capital. The man went back home with an order for the motorisation of his indispensable conveyance.

A Cot and a Couple of Earrings

C. S. Arunchand of Sai Bhavan (Sreekaryam, Trivandrum) eagerly wished to study computer science. He planned to join Government VHS School,

Vattiyoorkavu. He was selected at the interview but did not have the money to meet the initial expenses at school. The family rallied together to raise the necessary funds. They sold off their only cot; it fetched 500 rupees. His mother's earrings were pawned for 1,000 rupees.

On the following day, Arunchand went to the school, with the money but by then the school authorities had admitted some other pupil in his place. Arun had not applied to any other school and he did not have the financial backing to pursue studies in a private school.

Arun and his mother approached the CM with their appeal. OC gave the instructions; Arun was admitted in the same Vattiyoorkavu school. The CM's Office paid his fees. The CM gave him 1,000 rupees so that he could buy his uniform, textbooks, etc. Arun had got 546 marks (out of 600) for his SSLC.

Prabhodhini's Sister

The late Shyam S. Prabhodhini was an adventurous swimmer. His sister Mekha was given a job at the Travancore Titanium Products Ltd. Trivandrum, at the CM's initiative. Shyam had been a recipient of many honours; the most memorable among them was the inclusion of his name in the Limca Book of Records for having swum with his limbs tied. He died while training for further swimming exploits. His death was a severe blow to his poor family. Hence, it was imperative to grant his sister a job.

A Rescuer's Rescuer

In 1998, Lavanya rescued some of her friends from death. They had been on their way to college when she saw the other girls trapped between rails, and a train chugging towards them. Her sudden rescue operation was successful but she slipped and fell on the rails. The train ran over her, crushing and chopping her legs. Lavanya however, managed to fight back and walk again with the help of artificial limbs. She was determined to complete her studies, secure a job, and be independent. She sent in a request and the CM did not disappoint her. She was appointed to the post of LD Compiler in the Department of Statistics.

Pancharatna's Widowed Mother

In her first childbirth, Ramadevi presented her loving husband Premkumar with a rare gift of quintuplets. All five gems names began with the alphabet 'U': Uthra, Uthraja, Uthrajan, Uthara, and Uthama. Their home became the precious 'Pancharatna', an apt name in all ways. But their domestic bliss was short-lived. Premkumar could not make both ends meet and he ended his life in a debt trap. His house at Pothencode, Trivandrum, was now brimful of sighs and tears. The CM reached out to the hapless widow and her orphans. OC saw to it that Ramadevi was employed in the Pothencode branch of the Trivandrum District Co-operative Bank, and that the bank loans of her departed husband were written off.

A CM for the Downtrodden

As a public servant, OC has always had a soft place in his heart for the poor and the needy; he has a patient ear for their pleas and petitions; he has a knack for quick resolution of their problems.

Anyone could take their burdens to him, anytime, anywhere. It could be at his Jagathy residence, on his way to office in his car or even the CM's office in the Secretariat. No place was forbidden to anyone for an entry into OC's heart. Hundreds have been beneficiaries of his tenderness. Touching tales of his concern extended to all levels and classes no matter if they were the lowest of the low. OC's public life is full of such innumerable instances. So much so that the *Kerala Kaumudi* wrote when the OC government completed one year in office, 'You are the Chief Minister of all downtrodden people, Mr Oommen Chandy.'

In Problem Areas

As CM, OC once went to Kampakkallu, in Idukki district, a notorious place for plantations of Indian hemp (ganja). He had to travel by jeep for three hours along a rough forest road, and then walk for a full five hours and a half, on rougher terrain, during this historic visit. This rare event was telecast by NDTV, and covered by all other media.

He started on this ganja trail from Marayoor at 5.30 am on 23 May 2005. The CM was accompanied by a large retinue of officials from the police, excise, and forest departments, in 27 jeeps. They travelled for three hours through the Indira Gandhi Wildlife Sanctuary in Tamil Nadu, to reach Manchappetti. Very often the CM's Gypsy would be flung from one stone to another during this rugged ride. There was no bridge across the stream in the sanctuary. The Gypsy swam its way over the loosely scattered stones. It reached Manappetty Colony and then the party set out on their five-and-a-half hour tread up the 1,000- ft high Kampakkallu, a safe haven for ganja cultivators. They reached the spot by evening. The officials stayed there until the whole of the ganja crop was cut down and put to fire.

The CM's journey up there was undertaken in response to Poet Sugathakumari's demand, raised at the 'Sandalwood Meet' held at Marayur. It was pointed out that 800-odd acres of revenue land at Kadavary and Kampakkallu had been in full flower with the dreadful drug. The CM's visit led to a severe check on the ganja mafia in the state, and to the reclamation of the said thick forest land by the Department of Forests and Wild Life.

At Attappadi

The Attappadi Reserve Forest in the north of Kerala is home to several indigenous tribes who still practice age-old customs and rituals. A meeting was once held in the Secretariat Durbar Hall on the problems of the tribals. This was attended by many workers of various voluntary organisations, representatives of political parties, government officials, and others. Some of the Adivasis raised the problem of communication. Principal Secretary Ramanus Horro, of the Department of SC/ST Development, did not know Malayalam. They did not understand what he said nor did he follow what they said. It was no laughing matter though the cheerless complaint raised ripples of laughter.

After this meeting, the CM decided to visit Attappadi. He travelled all through the Adivasi region; the people were profoundly moved. OC was accorded a hero's welcome there and he had a meal with their chieftains. A three-member body was set up to study the problems of the Adivasis; Sugathakumari was on the committee. It was resolved that the government-owned 5085 acres in Wayanad, Aralam Farm, and Alankode would be distributed among the Adivasis within a stipulated time limit. The forest areas occupied by the Adivasis before 1 January 1980, would be registered as theirs, and deeds of ownership issued to them.

OC felt deeply disturbed when he returned from Attappadi. The Adivasis were among the most miserably marginalised sections of the community. According to the 2001 census, there were 3.64 lakh tribals in Kerala. That was 1.14 per cent of the state's population. When would they advance to the forefront of public life? It would have been much better if the money spent for their welfare had been distributed directly among them in cash.

Endosulfan Exiled

The CM visited Kasargode when the region was plagued by the Endosulfan pesticide. He decided to ban the deadly thing.

For years Endosulfan had been in use on the cashew estates of the Plantation Corporation at Periya Kasargode, owned by the state government. However, the pesticide brought with it inhuman tragedy. Its ill-effects led to insufferable wretchedness with steep rise reported in figures of children born with severe birth defects, still births, other physical handicaps and so on. OC visited some of these doomed dwellings. He spoke to the afflicted families. Their tears touched him to the quick. He was haunted by their tearful tales. The Cabinet met on 8 December 2004, and determined to ban Endosulphan for the good of the land and the people. The decision was diluted later. Endosulfan is still a burning issue in Kerala.

Among the Emigrants

The Malayalees have gone global. In the last five decades, the employment opportunities created in the state have been far from sufficient. Today we have our share of rice and curry thanks mostly to the lonely sweat of the Gulf Malayalees.

In OC's short spell as CM, he visited the Gulf region twice. For more than three decades emigrant Indians, especially those in the Gulf countries, have been clamouring for cheaper air-travel. OC went about to make this happen. On 29 April 2005, the Air-India 'Budget Express' landed in Abu Dhabi; it made real the demand for international flight at reduced rates. Hundreds of emigrant Indians heartily welcomed this maiden flight. The CM was on board that flight. It was with difficulty that the crowds there were held in check; they were alight with joy, and bore OC on their jubilant shoulders.

Generally, leaders go abroad for holidays. OC however maintained a busier schedule on these trips. He visited the Gulf for two days. He was with the people there from six in the morning till three am on the following day, listening to their manifold problems, addressing them at various gatherings and visiting the various places where these men turned their blood and sweat into gold for those back home.

The labour camps in Dubai were a piteous sight. OC visited those camps at Sonapur at 10 in the night. The Malayalee labourers led him to one of their rooms there. It was a mere 20 sq ft space to accommodate six men. Many of the men had been deprived of their wages for several months. They had paid huge amounts to the recruiting agents in Kerala, or elsewhere in India, with great expectations. The CM was deeply moved by the distressing conditions of these camps. He took up the matter with the Dubai authorities. It eased the situation. The companies paid up the overdue wages. The labourers could now complain to the local police if a company continued to deny their dues beyond three months. Earlier, they had to go to the Labour Department and there was no other refuge. The Dubai Government set up a Human Rights Cell. This was the highlight of all the steps taken.

There were several Malayalees in Dubai jails. OC wanted to visit them but the Indian Embassy would not let him. Most of the prisoners were behind the bars for what would be petty violations in Kerala, disobeying traffic rules, seeing video films, drinking etc. There were quite a number of prisoners who had been led into the trap by deceitful travel agents; among those cheated were several women too. The CM issued orders to inquire into the operations of such treacherous rackets in Kerala.

Joseph's Release

The CM's visit to Dubai led to the release of Joy Joseph (of Koikal, Puthupally, Kottayam) from prison. Joseph had been a machine operator in a concrete mixing company in Rashidiya, Dubai. He accidentally committed a crime that ended him up in jail. He had moved the concrete mixer which accidentally hit a worker behind him, and killed the man on the spot. He was a Senegalese. The court ordered Joseph to pay up two lakh dirhams; he could not pay up and was therefore imprisoned. He had no savings to support him. His company could not afford to pay the money, either. OC took up the matter with the company. The company promised to raise half the amount required. The other half was raised by Joseph's friends and well-wishers and the distressed soul was released. OC was doubly happy because they had been classmates once.

The Emigrants' Woes

All through his Gulf tour, OC repeatedly heard of two demands which needed his immediate attention. One was the emigrants' right to vote and the other had to do with their air-travel. The solution to both lay with the central government.

OC suggested to the Prime Minister and the External Affairs Minister that at least the emigrants on leave in India during the elections, should be allowed to exercise their suffrage. He went to Delhi with all the legal issues worked out regarding the measures to be taken in a democracy for permitting their emigrants to vote. The Central Cabinet discussed the issue, introduced the bill for the same at the Parliament Budget meeting in February 2006, and passed it in 2010. It will profit nearly five million Indian's abroad. For the first time NRIs are given a say in the process of governance in their homeland. Defence Minister A. K. Antony and Overseas Minister Vayalar Ravi played an important role in fulfilling this long cherished dream of the NRIs.

Air-India started a 'Budget Express' with a view to easing the travel expenses of the Gulf Malayalees. They could avail a maximum of 50 per cent reduction of rates in tickets. The airline however, was accused of giving a raw deal to the passengers. The tickets were withheld at times, or the flights cancelled outright. OC thought of floating a budget airline under the control of the Government of Kerala. It was named 'Air-Kerala'. The Nedumbassery Airport Company was given the charge of it. 'Air- Kerala' was to find 200 crores for its capital. The Government of Kerala was to hold 26 per cent of its shares. Its aim was to provide air travel facilities for the Gulf Malayalees at concessional rates. OC was shocked to hear that many of his compatriots abroad had not seen their homeland for 10 to 15 years; they simply could not afford the return tickets. Such people were to get 15 seats reserved for them. The Air-India Maharaja blocked their way. It was pointed out that a new airways company had to have a minimum fleet of 20 planes, and five years' experience flying in the domestic sector before it could seek permission to fly in the international one.

At the end of 2005 Asianet conducted an SMS survey to find Kerala's most popular leader of the year. OC was first while V. S. Achuthanandan was second. The votes of the emigrant Malayalees determined OC's position.

At the request of a large number of Malayalees residing in the USA, OC visited the country.. He was very warmly welcomed. He was the guest of honour at a certain dinner hosted by them. It was then that OCs sense of humour came to the fore. He listened to various comments by the diners.

'Kerala is peaceful these days.'

'There aren't many bundhs and hartals.'

'No killings or quarrels.'

'The people have become more cultured and civilised.'

'Everybody is engaged in some activity or other.'

OCs retort came quick and sharp, 'Oh yah! Its true...Kerala has become more cultured and peaceful now. It is because all the troublemakers have left Kerala. They are now in places like this.'

When the Tsunami Struck the State

The tsunami of 26 December of 2004 robbed 236 Malayalee lives; 176 from within Kerala, and 60 from outside the state. 4,055 houses were destroyed; 9,585 dwelling places were partially destroyed; 219 villages were laid waste. Roads, bridges, and power supply were severely damaged. The destruction cost the state 2,377 crores.

When the tsunami traumatised the coasts of Kerala at noon on that dismal December day, OC was at Adoor in Pathanamthitta District. T. K. Devakumar MLA, called him when it struck at Arattupuzha in Alleppy. OC hurried to the place. By three in the afternoon he reached Kayamkulam. Dead bodies had been sent to the government hospital there. Wailing relatives had surrounded the place. Kayamkulam, Valiyazheekkal, Cherthala, Anthakaranazhi, and other coastal areas were appallingly overpowered by distress, inexpressible and inconsolable. Kerala's 590 km long coastline was mortally shaken. The whole state felt the tremors.

When the news reached that the horrendous waves had committed graver atrocities in Quilon, OC rushed there. The corpses of Alappad had filled all the private hospitals in Ochira, and the government hospital at Karunagappally. Sobs, sighs, and screams rent the briny air. OC visited all these places. He had not the heart to the see the dead bodies of children there. Kerala had never experienced the tsunami before. The CM was shocked and saddened beyond measure, having looked into the jaws of death and destruction. It took some time for him to regain his usual composure.

He had given directions from Quilon to the Chief Secretary and the DGP to open a control room in Trivandrum to tackle the situation. Finance Minister Vakkom Purushothaman was asked to regulate stormy affairs there. He ordered a 9 pm Crisis Management Committee meeting in the capital. The Navy and the Coastguard were contacted for immediate assistance. When the Crisis Management Committee met, everybody felt sure that they had to face a wartime condition. They had to fight to prevail over the evil perpetrated by an aggressive nature. The people had to rise to the occasion and rally together to help one another. They drew up an action plan.

That day the CM reached home very late. The heart-rending sighs and tears of the people haunted his sleepless nights and restless days to follow. For days on end, the routine was set: Cabinet meeting in the morning followed by a visit to the tsunami-stricken places in the afternoon. Quick decision and immediate execution specially marked the conduct of the government in those anguished days.

The people of Azheekal and Kochida lamented that many lives could have been saved if there were bridges there. Orders were issued at once for the construction of those two bridges. The mothers of Arattupuzha raged that walls along the seashore would have safeguarded the little ones from the raging sea. The contractors had abandoned the construction work there. Orders were issued for the resumption of the erection of walls there. On many days the CM spent his time in the refugee camps late into the night. On one such visit, it was found that the government decisions had not been put into effect at the Kayamkulam relief camp. The District Collector had not even been to the place; he was transferred with immediate effect.

Prime Minister Manmohan Sigh visited the affected regions and he declared financial help to the tune of 246 crores. President Abdul Kalam sent a message that the whole nation was with the state. Congress President Sonia Gandhi repeatedly contacted Kerala government to affirm her solidarity. Malayalees all over the world condoled with their fellow beings in their homeland. They extended their timely help in cash and kind.

The central government warned the state of a probable re-appearance of the tsunami. The harrowing word came at 9 pm on 30 December 2004. The CM was in his office; he had not yet recovered from his earlier shock. The Delhi message caused mayhem. The CM called for an emergency meeting of the ministers and the top brass of the bureaucracy. The media poured in to the CM's office.

As the night deepened, the possibility of a tsunami waned considerably. The agony was abated. Alert caution was to be kept till 3 am. When it was past midnight, and nothing untoward had been reported, everyone else returned home. OC did not; the CM could not. He remained in his office, keeping vigil, until 3 am finally came.

As an administrator OC faced the greatest challenge of his tenure in CM's Office when the question of the post-tsunami rehabilitation came up.The first phase of the reconstruction was more or less satisfying. But then controversies started to rage and roar in Quilon where 2,969 houses were destroyed in the natural calamity. The number of applications for redress was 10 times that number. When the Collector attempted to do the survey to ascertain the number, many objected to it. Likewise, affected people were reluctant to leave the shoreline and build their dwellings towards the interior.

The Question of Diverted Expenses

An accusation was levelled against the OC government that the Tsunami Relief Funds were diverted. It had to do with a sum of 8 crore rupees. All funds, including the Tsunami Relief Funds, were routed through the CM's Relief Fund. From the day the tsunami struck on 26 December 2004, to the ending of the Tsunami Relief Funds collection on 17 June 2005, 37.50 crores was received into the CM's Relief Fund. The Tsunami Relief Fund was not permanent one and hence this manner of remittance. Until 8 December 2005, 29.14 crores was allotted for tsunami relief activities.

From the CM's Relief Fund, 8.3 crores was spent for other humanitarian care. This was taken for diverted expenses. In fact, of this amount, 4.73 crores was allotted for medical aid for the poor. The rest of the money was utilised for helping the victims of social disturbances, relief of 50,000 rupees each to 195 farmer families where the head of the family had committed suicide because he could not repay his debts, distributing free ration to the labourers on tea estates which had been locked out, and to the starving bamboo workers.

This expenditure was not a diversion of the Tsunami Relief Funds. It was not made available by taking away from the Tsunami funds, either. Nor was this money ill used. Let the people decide the right and wrong of it. That was OC's well-considered stand in the matter.

Peethambaran and Maniamma

Another controversy had it that adequate compensation was not given to a couple, Peethambaran and Maniamma, residing in the Fourth Ward of Azheekkal, Alappad Panchayat, Quilon. The pair was injured, and their two grandchildren swept away to their death, when the tsunami struck ashore. The aged couple were admitted into the Medical College Hospital, Trivandrum, for special attention. It was reported in the papers that their medication was unduly delayed.

The CM took note of it, granted them 10,000 rupees, and instructed the Medical College Hospital authorities to do the needful for them.

With the tsunami onslaught they had lost their house. After their hospital stay the couple went to stay in one of the temporary tents at Azheekkal. The Lokayukta observed that the said pair had not received fair relief and rehabilitation facilities. When he heard this, the CM sought the Quilon Collector's report. The Collector reported that Peethambaran and Maniamma, and their sons Jays and Jayakumar, had received 15.41 lakh rupees in addition to1.21 lakh rupees for medical expenses.

The Peethambaran–Maniamma question came up at the CM's Cabinet briefing. The *Kerala Kaumudi* reporter, who raised the question, was asked to look into the matter; the CM was prepared to appoint him as a one-man commission for it. The CM wrote a long detailed letter to all the media on this topic placing the facts and figures of the case. It came to a convincing conclusion. The Lokayukta conducted an adalat in Quilon and granted compensation to all who had assembled there. This stirred up another nest of hornets.

The Taming of the Media

All the channels were given a special interview when OC had completed 100 days as CM. The Ice-cream Scandal (The Ice Cream Scandal was antoher sex scandal that rocked Kerala. One the most prominent hance implicated in it was of P. K. Kunhalikutty. Leader of the Muslim Leauge and Minister in Oommen Chandy's Cabinet) had by then become hot stuff which nearly melted away the UDF government's 100 days achievements. The CM held on to the axiom that the law would take its own course. T. N. Gopakumar of Asianet led his interview to the 'ice-cream' trap.

'If Oommen Chandy were in Kunhalikutty's shoes what would he do?' was his barbed question.

'That would depend on each person who had to take the decision.' The CM gave an evasive reply.

Gopakumar pulled the net closer. He faced the camera, and declared to the viewers that OC would surely have an opinion of his own in the matter, and would now share the same with them. The memorable retort came after the lapse of a moment or two.

'The people of this state know better than me what I would do if I were in that position.'

Asianet highlighted that revealing quote in their newscast over and over again that day.

Cartoonists and caricaturists find OC's face quite facile for their oblique lines. Long nose, dishevelled hair, torn shirt, thick moustache–details that endear themselves to the caricaturists pen.

It is over four decades since the media and he have forged a relationship. OC has always been on friendly terms with them. They include the Left Front journalists and reporters. Anyone's call would be attended to and everyone was welcome to jab him with their queries and inquiries. He would attend their meetings and festivities but never did he go to them with a request that his news be flashed, splashed, or published. Smaller dailies used to approach him for government ads; OC would take a considerate attitude towards them. The money paid to a large establishment would be enough to pay several small ones together. Quite a few of the latter were struggling to pull on. The ads could be a boon to them.

The media's absolute support went a long way to ensure the success of OC's Mass Contact Programme. But when more than half the districts had been covered came the rub from the 'Ice-cream Parlour'. Meanwhile some members of the media were manhandled at Karipur Airport and the Indiavison Office in Cochin was stormed. The media began to keep a distance from the CM and the government. They took out a protest march to the spot where the Mass Contact Programme was being held in Trivandrum. They led another march to Cliff House, the official residence of the Finance Minister Vakkom Purushothaman when the UDF High-

Power Committee met there. Vakkom and the media had a go at each other. OC, 'Media's Darling', had to risk his epithet, in the battle.

When the OC government completed 100 days, some editors were served a dinner in New Delhi. This caused a controversy. The journalists from Kerala had been left out from that party. Forty leading editors of Delhi were invited to it. Usually reporters are not invited to parties thrown for editors. The purpose of the said party was to give a national introduction to OC as a Kerala CM who was determined to woo investors. After the press conference OC left. The get-together was arranged on the rooftop of the Oberoi, in the biting cold of an evening in December. It was alleged that alcohol was served there. The media came out with all the details including the hotel bills. There was no bill for alcohol served as there was no such item was on the menu at all.

The CM always conferred with the media at the briefing that followed the Cabinet meeting every Wednesday. When the Cabinet decisions were put forward, there would be questions on current issues. OC's press conferences were witty and vivacious because they would brim with stinging queries and surprising retorts. The CM hardly ever avoided a question from the media. Surely, he would occasionally pull a tantrum or two. He would pretend not to have caught a taunting point, or ask the reporters to repeat themselves, to gain time and think through the answer. He might say that he would look into the matter, or that it had not been brought to his notice. On the whole, they were free to question him about anything, anytime, anywhere.

OC would manage the media with a great deal of ease. Most of his answers had the backing of facts and figures that he quoted for the verity and worth of his words. He was too busy to make a detailed analysis of the newspapers every day. However, he has such a wealth of experience that it is not that easy for the media and their ilk to catch him unawares.

OC had to face the media with folded hands thrice: the Ice-cream Parlour controversy, the Devaswom Board corruption charges, and the Health Minister's resignation.

Generally speaking, OC has always been tolerant towards adverse criticism in both the print and visual media, and elsewhere. There were very painful instances, too. After one and half hours of interview with the CM, *India Today* came out with the cover story, titled 'Oommen Chandy Failed, 20 out of 100'. It was on the 100th day of OC as CM. They ranked OC as the worst CM of the country. Gujarat Chief Minister Narendra Modi was their best!

A Journey by the Amrita Express

Questions were raised at a press conference regarding the CM's 'controversial' journey by the Amrita Express. Two weeklies joined hands together in maligning OC, and published articles on this non-issue. It was character assassination of the most despicable kind!

The grapevine had it that OC, before he assumed the CM's office, travelled to Trichur by the Trivandrum–Palghat Amrita Express that departed from the capital at 11 pm, accompanied by an unidentified woman. *Exclusive,* a weekly from Palghat gave lead in this scurrilous gossip. *Malayalam,* a weekly, owned by *The Indian Express* Group, took up the thread of this lame slander. It came out with an inappropriate cover picture as well. Certain dailies carried forward this empty canard. At the cabinet briefing, this topic was raised. The CM paused for a moment and then came the dramatic reply:

'Yes, there was a woman with me on that night train to Palghat.' A stunned silence prevailed but OC was not done. Then came the devastating addition.

'She was my wife.'

His wife, Mariamma Oommen, is an officer with Canara Bank. She was on her way to Trichur for the Women's Day Conference; her husband had accompanied her. OC was prepared to provide the relevant proofs for the same. He urged all the media of the state to conduct an open enquiry into the identity of his travelling partner. Nobody bothered to follow suit. OC's word was the voice of truth. Some urged him to go to court for the libel. He ignored that advice.

Any man would wither away in such a scandalous circumstance. OC's integrity emerged the brighter for the wagging tongues of tainting calumny. The Amrita Express episode proved that anything could flame up into controversy in Kerala. OC was not afraid of such malicious mockery of freedom. Hence his staunch stand when the Smart City issue was burning bright in the media.

Since he was very busy, the CM gave only a few interviews to the media. Most of his media interactions were held in the dead of the night. OC had a thesis on the way the media often followed the policy of planting negative news. He would say, 'They want controversies; and these they would treat as news.' A dozen-odd channels and umpteen papers and magazines are vying with one another to survive in the state, and prevail. The air is charged with their cut and thrust. This cut-throat competition induces baseless reports, unfounded controversies, and all kinds of groundless gimmicks solely to keep themselves abreast of things, and head over shoulders above their peers.

OC, as CM, was often the focus of these contentions and controversies. He knew very well that the poisoned arrow was aimed at the CM, and not at OC, the person.

The Cynosure of the Assembly

A couple of people once came to the spectators' gallery of the Assembly to observe the proceedings there. The bell rang for voting. The CM ran from his adjacent room to the Assembly Hall. The two spectators ran outside; they thought some accident had occurred in the Assembly. They were first time visitors, of course.

This was OC's time-honoured way. When the bell rang for voting, he would rush to the Hall. His absence would not matter; the Ruling Front had a huge majority in the House. He has tried his best to attend all the sessions of the Assembly. This did not change when he assumed the CM's office. However, crowds would gather around him whether the session was on or not. What with visitors, conferences, and meetings, his room in the Assembly complex would be as busy as a beehive.

There have been very many dramatic moments in OC's Legislative life. The summit of them all must have been when he stood up in the House to reply to the No-confidence Motion against his government that cropped up in July 2005. The Opposition had insisted on three days of discussion. OC had agreed to it. The discussions were telecast, live. Many concluded that the government was in a fix indeed. Deputy Leader of the Opposition, Kodiyeri Balakrishnan, presented 13 items for the basis of the motion but the discussions slipped into an entirely different matter—the SNC Lavalin case, the bête noire of the Opposition.

The Opposition came up with a list of charges, such as the defeat in the by-elections in Azheekode and Koothuparambu, to show that the government had lost the people's support; they had lost their unity; they had not fulfilled their election promises; they had deceived the unemployed youth; the religious minorities felt unprotected; the Tsunami Relief Fund had been misappropriated; corruption was rampant. OC went deep into the question of bribery and corruption, especially in high places.

Twenty-five hours of discussion filled with unsparingly scathing criticism, protracted into three days! OC and Electricity Minister Aryadan Muhammed had prepared in detail to answer the Lavalin question. Their homework could do the trick. The CM and his Cabinet came to the House with confidence writ large on their faces.

Revenue Minister K. M. Mani observed that the Opposition's charges were like the debtor's account kept at a local tea-shop. PWD Minister, M. K. Muneer turned very emotional. He said that he felt dispirited after the Opposition's baseless accusations. Ministers Thiruvanchoor Radhakrishnan, Adoor Prakash, and Ramachandran Master spoke up in good earnest and then it was Aryadan Muhammed's turn.

Aryadan's Lavalin Mastery!

The Ruling Bench urged Aryadan on. That day the Opposition was an army in total disarray, without a commanding general. Opposition Leader V. S. Achuthanandan was for blacklisting Lavalin Company; Dr Thomas Isaac, however, opposed the move. The others had not been prepared for the defence. It required much technical study.

Aryadan countered the Opposition charge that Congress Minister G. Karthikeyan had initiated the contract with Lavalin for consultancy service regarding the renovation of certain hydro-electric projects. He said that it was during Pinarayi Vijayan's tenure as Power Minister that Lavalin was given a supply contract for these projects and at an exorbitant rate and moreover, the renovation work had proved a failure. Along with that, the company had given an assurance that they would be through with the first phase of the Kannur Cancer Centre's construction in 2000, and that a year later they would see through its second phase. They had slowly but surely withdrawn from their word.

The contract regarding the Cancer Centre was made between Lavalin and the Government of Kerala. This was not mentioned in the contract made between Lavalin and the Kerala State Electricity Board (KSEB). The money that the Board owed the company for the renovation works, had to be paid; no part of it could be recovered or held back. Any arbitration regarding the same could be carried out only in Paris. This would mean great financial liability for the government, Aryadan pointed out. He concluded that the Lavalin affair was one of the biggest corruption deals in the country.

He took nearly an hour to expand on the topic. He depended on the Lavalin records for authority. Kodiyeri Balakrishnan led the Opposition battle. Whenever Dr Thomas Isaac stood up in the House, Aryadan silenced him with the mention of Richard Franke, his American connection that smelt of rotten fish.

OC's Turn

It was then OC's turn. He sifted relevant details out of the vigilance enquiry into the Lavalin deal, and hit the Opposition hard with corruption charges in it. When the Subject Committee had met on 11 January 2002, its Chairman was the then Water Resources Minister T M Jacob; Kodiyeri Balakrishnan was a member. The committee had found quite a few irregularities in the Pallivasal, Chenkulam, and Panniyar renovation works. On their recommendations, a vigilance enquiry had been initiated, OC observed. (T. M. Jacob and his Kerala Congress faction was with the LDF at that time. They later merged with Karunakaran's DICK [Democratic Indira Congress Karnunakaran]. He later revived his party and joined UDF and were seated on the Opposition benches).

V. S. Achuthanandan interrupted OC's speech. OC promised to refer the case to the CBI if he wanted it that way. The Lavalin case was already with the Vigilance Department and they were going through the 7,000 pages of the case file. Though it would take quite some time to go through them, the vigilance enquiry would be made within a set time limit, declared OC, concluding the Lavalin question for the day.

The rest of his speech was reserved for breaking the point of every accusation levelled against his government. The mountain had shrunken into a molehill, and was removed before long.

OC let loose his volleys. 'If there is a 3,000 crores corruption to be considered, spell it out clearly and courageously. There is nothing wrong about it. I have been in this House for the last 35 years. Until today nobody has voiced any charges of corruption against me. I don't mean to say that the Opposition Leader has no right to accuse me on any score. If he does so, it must be done with due seriousness. Not in a silly, indifferent manner. Let me tell my dear members of the Opposition. Today your leader handed over to me a small chit of paper. It was not even torn from his letter pad. Just a casual piece of paper as would be used at a local tea-shop to scribble a customer's bill on. It was indeed meant to be an accusation against my government's corruption to the tune of 2,416 crores.

Well, my dear sir, couldn't you be a bit serious in such matters of importance? Couldn't you, please, make use of the stationery, the staff, and other facilities that the Honourable Leader of the Opposition enjoys at the state's expense? Now let the people see it for themselves. (Here the CM raised the bit of paper in the sight of all in the House.) Is this the way such an accusation should be brought to the notice of the government?'

OC went on to counter all the accusations one by one, advancing the necessary proof for each item. These were shown to have either been done by the preceding LDF government or ushered in by them. Regarding the fees in the self-financing colleges, OC asked how many children of the Opposition members were studying in such institutions. He had collected a complete list of them. He narrated how the Fashion City authorities from Singapore and BMW authorities from Germany had to return home without even holding discussions because of an LDF-sponsored hartal; how the officials of the National Waterways, whom K. S. Manoj MP (for Alleppey) had invited to the town for talks regarding the terminal for the Nehru Trophy Boat Race, were forced to return to Delhi because of a strike; how former Justice V. R. Krishna Iyer had written to Sitaram Yechury, CPM Politburo member, against the innumerable and irresponsible bundhs and hartals in Kerala.

OC's speech that day took an hour and a half. It was neatly rounded off with a declaration that all Kerala saw and heard eagerly. Just as the state employees received their salary, all the 15 lakh people here would be paid their welfare pensions precisely on the first of every month though it meant a deduction of 18 crore rupees on the exchequer. Until it was paid, he would not take a single paisa by way of salary. Finance Minister Vakkom Purushothaman observed that the cheque for the welfare pensions would be given on the very first of every month, and that the CM's salary would not be delayed for it.

The No-confidence Motion was crushed and defeated. The ruling benches showered congratulations on the CM. On the floor of the House, and in the hearts of the people at large, OC won a thumping victory. Indiavision's opinion poll saw the government advancing at 70: 30. It was a defining moment in OC's Assembly life!

When the 11th Legislative Assembly's last session took place in February 2006, OC attended only the very last day of the budget session since he was convalescing after the accident at Davos. He made a short speech while taking part in the discussions on expenditure. He said that the UDF had forced CPM State Secretary Pinarayi Vijayan to take out a procession through the entire length of Kerala, from the northern tip to the southern end of the state, with a motto on the need of comprehensive development. He requested everyone to cooperate with the implementation of Vision 2010. The CM had reached the House with the help of a walker and a pair of crutches.

Scandals and Allegations

On 18 October 2004, Regina, a party to the Ice Cream Parlour Case, came out with some scandalous allegations against Industries Minister P. K. Kunhalikutty. The event was flashed by the Indiavision news channel. Regina was just repeating her charges that she had revealed in 1997 when the LDF had been in power. These had been covered by the papers but now the audiovisual publicity, of course, enhanced its intensity. The minister was in Mumbai on his way to Saudi Arabia for the Umra. He flew to Mecca only after ascertaining the news himself. In the days that followed, Indiavision and other channels highlighted the scenes of Regina going from place to place with her infant. Indiavision's rating rose overnight!

After the Umra, Kunhalikutty landed at Karipur Airport where a dozen media persons were manhandled during the 'heroic welcome' accorded to him by his ardent followers. The media went on a war path. Wherever Kunhalikutty went, they appeared wearing black badges, and mouthing 'Murdabad' slogans.

At Taj Hotel, Cochin, Kunhalikutty was besieged by the media; and the police confronted them. The clash continued for hours. The Left Front supporters rallied around the media people. It was with great difficulty, the security personnel got the minister out of the hotel. As he was getting into a car, someone cast a piece of black cloth at him; and it landed on his head. That photo made the front page of most newspapers the next morning.

Meanwhile, another case of sexual harassment was creating ripples in the state. The victim was Shari S. Nair (17), who died on 13 November 2004. The case had been referred to the CBI before her demise. V. S. Achuthanandan had stated that the girl had burst into tears when a VIP visited her in the hospital. He had promised that if the LDF came to power, the culprits would be booked. It is a pity that the identity of the VIP remains unknown to this day.

In the capital, the Thamarakshan group of the RSP (Revolutionary Socialist Party) trooped out a march that turned violent. Several media people got beaten up there. They and the police entered into an open fray that lasted till midnight.

The High Court had imposed a stay order on the Ice-cream Parlour case that arose after Regina's disclosures. At first, the woman had mentioned the name of Kunhalikutty. Then she said she did not know anyone named Kunhalikutty. There were 16 accused in the case. The witnesses went back on their testimonies. All the accused were acquitted in January 2006.

The welcome that Kunhalikutty had been accorded in Kannur by the Muslim League followers had turned violent. Because of the unruly state within the Assembly, the proceedings had to be abandoned the very day itself. Outside the Assembly, things were no better. The capital city had the look of a battleground. The Congress High Command had woken up to the gravity of the situation. OC flew to Delhi, and conferred with Sonia Gandhi.

On 16 December, the 100-Day Action Drive Programme was successfully rounded off. The same day, OC's Amrita Express Journey' appeared in some papers. On 26th, the tsunami shocked the shores of Kerala. On 28th, Kunhalikutty tendered his resignation which ended a political tsunami. OC was on the defensive in this affair, right from the beginning. On 6 January 2005, Kunhalikutty's confidant Ibrahim Kunju was sworn in as the new Industries Minister.

IT Chief Minister

The IT Department used to be the CM's portfolio. At the inception of the UDF ministry, the Muslim League leader Panakkad Shihab Thangal insisted on getting the department for them. The Congress did not oppose it since the experienced administrator Kunhalikutty was to chair it. The case was different with Ibrahim Kunju, a newcomer to the ministry and the Muslim League did not object to it, either.

Those were days when talks had started on Dubai Internet City establishing Smart City in Cochin. The CM presided over the destiny of this project. The Left Front and a section of the media were against the move. Certain papers that had much influence in the Gulf region, took an opportunistic stand; they supported the venture there but opposed it in Kerala. The CM was very particular that projects and programmes for the good of the people should not be toppled by controversies. He answered articles with articles, and statements with their own kind. Kerala had never witnessed a development programme causing such a media war.

T. M. Jacob laid the accusation in the Assembly that Baji George, Chief Operating Manager, Dubai Internet City, was operating as OC's agent.

The CM had talks with the Opposition Leader as well as the leaders of the Left-Front Parties. Further charges were that Dubai Internet City was a private company, and that the deal had brought OC a bribe of 500 crores. The CM fought on all fronts to maintain his innocence.

The On-line Lottery Ban

Another controversy had to do with the abolition of all lotteries, including Kerala's paper lottery. Many blind and physically challenged individuals, among others, who made their living by selling lotteries, marched down the streets in loud protest against the ban. However, the on-line lottery had caused a social havoc in the state; it had to be abolished. They had approached the Supreme Court against the segregation and the court's verdict favoured them. So the government was forced to dispense with all lotteries. What had been done in good earnest had a sad end. The abolition was repealed. Legislation was made to do away with the on-line lottery alone. A big social evil was evicted from Kerala for good.

Minister Viswanathan's Resignation

On 8 February 2005, the High Court criticised Forests Minister K. P. Viswanathan, to the effect that the minister had direct contact with the culprits of the Sandalwood Case (The case related to the large-scale smuggling of sandalwood and allied products from Mariyoor and other reserved forests in the state to the Valayar Rural Industries in Palghat district). The court added that things had come to a pretty pass that the sandalwood mafia could avail themselves of any government order in their favour.

The Assembly was in session when such remarks were made by the High Court. The press revelled in revealing the same in column after column. The Opposition moved the House with an adjournment motion demanding the resignation of Viswanathan. While he was explaining the notice, the minister dramatically declared his resignation. He referred to the High Court's observations as the unkindest cut of all. He would keep away until the court clarified everything related to the case. The case dragged on. After 10 months, A. Sujanapal took over the portfolio from Thiruvanchoor Radhakrishnan who had run it alongside his own Water Resources Department. Thiruvanchoor had gone about it splendidly. So much so, that Sugathakumari and others requested that Forests and Wild Life portfolio should not be taken away from his charge. Later, when Ramachandran Master resigned, the Health Ministry became an additional portfolio for Thiruvanchoor again.

After five years Viswanathan was exonerated by the Supreme Court. Justice was delivered at last, but too late for any ministerial recompense.

Ramachandran Master's Resignation

The new KPCC and the new welfare projects of the government were slowly winning back the people's support. But unsavoury gossip circulating in the Health Ministry ended in Minister Ramachandran Master's resignation in January 2006. It had much to do with the CM's decision to transfer the Pollution Control Board from the Health Ministry to the Department of Environment, and to hand over the charge of it to A. Sujanapal. This was done on the basis of a Subject Committee report.

On 4 January, Ramachadran Master had, in haste, tendered his resignation, thinking that his portfolio was to be taken over by the CM. He did not attend the Cabinet meeting and remained in his office room. His staff had leaked the news of it to the media. When he realised that the move was to affect only the Pollution Control Board, he withdrew his resignation in greater haste!

Meanwhile the Lokayukta had come to receive many complaints regarding appointments and transfers in the Health Department. One of the complaints was that the Minister and his APS P. Radhakrishnan had threatened some of the complainants. The Lokayukta referred this in writing to the CM. The CM asked IG Senkumar to look into the matter and make a report on it. The IG found that the accusations against the minister were baseless but not those against the APS. The CM asked the minister to sack the man from his staff. All those details were reported to the Lokayukta. It provoked the Lokayukta. He took exception to the IG's enquiry; he found it parallel to his own, and quite insulting to his high office. He pointed out that even the CM came under the purview of the Lokayukta, and that the CM had no sense of the law.

On the report of the IG, the CM sought to justify the Health Minister. He was to address a press conference to this effect at 4 pm on 13 January when Ramachandran Master was boomeranged by his own words. The Minister had contacted the Wyanad DMO that day. His mobile phone conversation with the DMO was recorded and flashed by Kairali TV that very afternoon. The last part of his 73 second conversation was as follows, 'If anybody approaches you hereafter, say that you have not given such a statement, that you do not know what has been recorded, and that you said things in a hurry. Understand?'

The Minister was obviously asking the DMO to change the statement that the latter had given to the Lokayukta. He had been caught in his own trap! The CM called him and Finance Minister Vakkom Purushothaman into his chamber. They conferred amongst themselves for an hour. The resignation was decided there and it was announced in the press conference that followed immediately after, the one press conference where OC could not be quite his cool self.

After Ramachandran Master's resignation, the CM proceeded to the next Cabinet briefing fully armed to mount an offensive regarding the comments of the Lokayukta. It was a calculated and calibrated offensive that he mounted to counter the flying arrows.

A Flawless Presentation

OC started the assault with a characteristic question to the media, 'What would you have done if you had been in my position?

I had received a report from the Lokayukta that the minister had threatened the witnesses. There were three options before me. One, take the necessary action on the basis of the Lokayukta's report, two, wait till further report arrived or three, get to know things on my own.

From the beginning, it was clear that I could not take any action merely on the basis of the Lokayukta's report for he had pointed out that no conclusion had been arrived at. Nor had any verdict been passed on the case. Waiting till the final report of the Lokayukta came, was another option. How could I? How could I sit still and wait so long in such a controversial case? The only option possible for me was to try and find out the facts of the case, on my own. Hence, my entrusting the enquiry with IG Senkumar. It was not a parallel enquiry into the case. The case before the Lokayukta was that the minister had threatened those who had given the statements. Action was taken immediately on getting the report.

I'm a commoner, and not exactly very intelligent. Please tell me why did the Lokayukta write such a letter to me? Until God and my people decide against me, I won't keep my mouth shut.' With these words OC concluded his impregnable defence.

Contrary to their usual practice, the media fell silent that day. The Indiavision carried out a survey: 'Was the CM right in asking the IG to conduct the inquiry?' 70 per cent of those who voted supported his stand.

There had been differences of opinion with the Lokayukta even before the Health Minister affair. The Lokayukta had taken a one-sided approach in the question of compensation for the tsunami victims of Quilon. After that, the government issued an order that the Government Guest Houses would not be made available for the Lokayukta's sittings. It was tit for tat, though the order had been based on the decision of the previous Left government.

OC vs Sukumar Azheekodu

A letter resolved the differences of opinion that had arisen between OC and Sukumar Azheekodu. The state government's greatest literary prize, the Ezhuthachan Award for 2004, was for Azheekode and the CM was to honour him with it. Meanwhile OC had agreed to inaugurate a multi-storeyed building erected near the Calicut Jail premises. Azheekodu declared that he would not receive the award from the CM because the construction of the building had violated the rules, and the CM should not have inaugurated it.

The CM humbly wrote to the indomitable litterateur. 'I am one of those very many who are happy that you are the recipient of this year's Ezhuthachan Award. I am not sure if you remember that I rang up the other day to congratulate you on that. I did, and do, believe that you have achieved your laurels without anyone's support or favour. And I also firmly believe that merit should be recognised and rewarded. I have gathered from the media that you would not receive the Ezhuthachan Award from me. That, of course, is a matter of your choice. I wholeheartedly believe that you should receive the award instituted in honour of Ezhuthachan, the Father of Malayalam. You have only to inform me from whom you'd receive that honour. I'll make the necessary arrangements for the same. Or else, it shall be brought home to yours if you'd have it thus.'

Azheekode was moved by OC's respectful reply. He agreed to receive the award from OC himself and he did so in the Durbar Hall of the Secretariat. Azheekode handed over the prize money of one lakh rupees to OC as a contribution to the CM's Relief Fund.

Wrangling and Bickering

The May 2001 Assembly elections had brought unexpected and unprecedented victory to the UDF. One hundred happy MLAs! Bickering had been rife even before the UDF ministry was formed. The Congress High Command had sent Gulam Nabi Azad and Motilal Vohra as their emissaries to decide on the Congress leader. K. Karunakaran insisted that his son K. Muraleedharan be made KPCC President if A. K. Antony was to be the new CM.

On 27 May 2001, AK was sworn in as CM. The same day, Muraleedharan replaced Thennala Balakrishna Pillai who was unceremoniously removed from the President's chair. At the formation of the council of ministers, again Karunakaran took a stern stand. He wanted K. V. Thomas to be inducted into the cabinet. AK was for OC. Karunakaran had his way. OC took charge as UDF Convener. The crisis in the Congress was diffused for the time being!

In this election OC had faced in Cherian Philip an unexpected rival in his Puthupally constituency. Cherian had for long been the custodian of OC's as well as AK's conscience. Now he had fallen out with the Congress, and the two leaders. He contested from OC's home constituency as a CPM Independent, and was defeated by a margin of 12,575 votes. He had raised a revolt because he had feared to lose the battle in Trivandrum East constituency that the Congress Party had assigned for him. But Congress and the UDF, represented by B Vijayakumar, won the seat with a margin of 14,068 votes.

The April 2003 elections to the two Rajya Sabha seats occasioned another commotion in the Congress in Kerala. Vayalar Ravi, a prominent Congress leader and Thennala Balakrishna Pillai were the official candidates. Karunakaran moved forward his own rival candidate, Kodoth Govindan Nair, President of Kasargode DCC. Kodoth could not make it and many cried for disciplinary action against him. He had bagged 26 votes, five of which were from UDF partners. OC had identified them. (When he donned the CM's cap he avoided their presence in the ministry.)

A Coup That Failed

The 'I' Group of the Congress attempted to overthrow the UDF

Government. The move was countered by timely manoeuvres. The group had planned to vote against the government during the debate in the Assembly on Supplementary Demands. If they succeeded, they could have defeated the Ruling Front. The government would have had to resign. Their design was clear from the fact that none of them had spoken in defence of the government when the debate had been on.

The 'Official Group' of the Congress, OC, Aryadan Muhammed, and others, racked their brains. A fax message arrived from the AICC; Speaker Vakkom Purushothaman was to disqualify four MLAs (P. P. George, Adoor Prakash, E. M. Agusthy, and Shobhana George) for having operated as election agents to Kodoth Govindan Nair, rival to the official candidate for the Rajya Sabha seat. That meant 'I' Group's 21 MLAs would be reduced to 17, less than one third of the total 63 MLAs. They would be unable to defy the whip and vote the government to defeat. The dramatic move silenced the group. Though the AICC fax was charged to be fraudulent, Ahmed Patel confirmed that he had dispatched it.

The group war saw another battlefront emerging when they had to decide on the Congress candidate for the Lok Sabha by-election in Ernakulam. The by-election had to be held because of the untimely demise of George Eden, the sitting MP, who had been in the 'I' group. The group was planning to field their own candidate, and to defeat the official candidate M. O. John (Municipal Chairman, Alwaye). Later they changed their stand, and worked for the Left Independent Sebastian Paul who saw victory with a margin of 22,132 votes. The seat had been the Congress Party's for years.

Karunakaran was in Ernakulam for the election campaign. The media asked him whether the UDF candidate would win. 'The television is a great contribution from Indiraji to this country. Don't forget that,' he said. That was Karunakaran's characteristic exercise in equivocation.

The TV was Sebastian Paul's election symbol!

Karunakaran and Muraleedharan clamoured for a change in the leadership; they sought to oust the CM. The other group asked for the removal of Muraleedharan from the KPCC President's chair. The leaders of the constituent parties of the UDF flew to Delhi in an effort to end the discord. Meanwhile the UDF candidate Elizabeth Mammen of Kerala Congress (M) won the by-election in Tiruvalla. The 'I' Group was again accused of having backed her Left rival during the electioneering.

Minister T. M. Jacob and R. Balakrishna Pillai suggested to the Congress High Command that Muraleedharan be made a minister. The Lok Sabha elections were round the corner; the 'I' Group applied greater pressure by demanding Muraleedharan be made Deputy Chief Minister, or Minister for Finance or Home Affairs. The anti-Karunakaran group banded together and they dispatched OC to Delhi. OC urged the High Command to take action against those who had disobeyed the dictates of the Congress Party during the Rajya Sabha elections, and the Assembly by-elections in Ernakulam and Tiruvalla. AK was for unity in the Congress Party, especially because the Lok Sabha elections were around the corner.

The Hint of a Division

The Karunakaran faction met at Tagore Theatre, Trivandrum, on 28 January 2004 and 19 MLAs attended it. Their leader declared that a new party was going to be floated. He added that if anybody from his group deserted him for a berth in the cabinet, they would have no place in his party. This formation of a new party was announced when the cabinet meeting had been on. It was 4 pm. The cabinet had met in the evening because the Assembly was in session. The 'I' Group Ministers P. Sankaran and Kadavoor Sivadasan had joined the meeting straight from the 'Rival Show'. Sankaran could not keep his overflowing heart in check. Muraleedharan was allowed to be inducted into the cabinet.

At the press conference that followed, AK expressed his optimism in all things. A query sought the sudden reason for the induction. He replied that he simply was an optimist always. He narrated the tale of Robert Bruce. He would not over-react and act in a manner that would break up the Congress Party and please those who wished to see it go splinters.

It appeared that Muraleedharan was content with the Ministry served to him. He announced his allegiance to Sonia Gandhi; he would not divide the party and hence there was a temporary cessation of hostilities.

Then Murali played truant; he would not join the cabinet unless he was offered an important portfolio. On the 11th day of his recalcitrance, he was sworn into office as the Power Minister after having resigned as MP and President, KPCC. The other ministers of the 'I' Group had to put up with a change of portfolio. Karunakaran blessed his son before the latter's swearing-in. Murali's successor, P. P. Thankachan assumed office as Acting President, KPCC.

The Congress Party and the UDF government were making preparations for the Lok Sabha elections. Their euphoria was short lived. Determining the candidacy of seat seekers was the first bone of contention. Padmaja (Karunakarna's daughter) wanted Mukundapuram seat which was claimed by P. C. Chacko. The Congress politics in Kerala fell into another dilemma.

AK and P. P. Thankachan flew to Delhi, undecided on a panel of 63 for 13 seats, out of the 17 allotted to the Congress Party. The sitting constituencies of Trivandrum, Adoor, Mavelikkara, and Trichur had found no contestants within the party. In Delhi, AK and Karunakaran met and discussed the election issue. They called on Sonia Gandhi. Later they issued a joint communiqué that the Congress in Kerala would remain united.

Meanwhile a Rajya Sabha seat fell vacant. Karunakaran was tipped for it, unopposed. In connection with the election procedures, he declared his assets to be 4,000 rupees in cash and a gold ring. Muraleedharan confessed his error in having tried to thwart the victory of the UDF candidates in the Ernakulam and Tiruvalla by-elections.

Lok Sabha Elections, 2004

13 May 2004 was indeed an unlucky day for the Congress Party. That was the day the results of the Lok Sabha elections were declared. The UDF lost all seats except the Muslim League's Ponnani. In the Assembly by-election in Vadakkanchery, Muraleedharan was defeated by a margin of 3,715 votes. The 2004 defeat for the Congress was worse than the 1967 Left sway; then they had got at least Panampilly Govinda Menon's Mukundapuram. In 2004, they drew an utter blank! The State Congress slipped into sad and somber silence. At the Centre, the Congress could lead a united front to rule the nation; they had 219 seats, the largest coalition available.

Sonia Gandhi was elected the leader of the party. Nevertheless, she declined the premiership of the government. That decision catapulted her to the pinnacle of heroism; her esteem increased among the leaders of the world. *Forbes* magazine elected her the third most powerful woman in the world.

The High Command Arrives

Margaret Alva and R. L. Bhatia arrived in Trivandrum as the High Command's representatives. They talked to around 300 people in three days, and returned to Delhi. Though MLAs had not demanded a change in leadership, the delegates reported that the ministry and the KPCC were to be reconstituted.

On 16 June 2004, R. L. Bhatia took over as Governor of Kerala. Cartoons appeared in the the State's dailies that he had been appointed Permanent Observer of the Congress affairs here. Thennala Balakrishna Pillai became President, KPCC, once again. The present appointment was, as it were, an act of reparation. An ad hoc committee was announced for the KPCC. Instead of the earlier 107 member mammoth committee, there were only 30. The extreme factionalists were excluded from it.

The Congress High Command decided to bring changes at the ministerial level as well. OC was summoned to take over the reign of the state. His 35 year-old parliamentary life reached its pinnacle and natural conclusion as far as his Kerala politics is concerned.

The Relentless Rallies

The Lok Sabha election fiasco and the cabinet reshuffle had staved off the divisive tendencies in the Congress Party. After a short break, the Congress politics in the state turned tumultuous. The bull ran amok again. 'I' Group resumed the push-pull power game. The Group's demand was that V. Balram be made Chairman of the KTDC. OC did not oblige. Balram had earlier resigned his Vadakkanchery Assembly seat for the sake of Muraleedharan. Padmaja had resigned as Chairman, KTDC, to contest in the Lok Sabha elections. The group threatened that they would hold rallies on the streets to push for their demands. Pranab Mukherjee and Ahmed Patel conferred with Karunakaran in Delhi but they could not resolve the issue. 'The rally was to be held because it had not been banned by the party. If it were banned, they would still hold a rally against the ban'. Karunakaran was firm on the point of holding the rally.

On 9 March 2005, his group took out their first rally in Calicut. Sixteen MLAs were brought there, to demonstrate their strength. On the day before the rally, Muraleedharan had been suspended from the party. He described OC as a dictator and criticised Ahmed Patel, Sonia Gandhi's Political Secretary, and the bridge between the Congress Party and the Central Government. He would not bow before an 'Aluminium Patel', Murali scorned, though he respected Sonia Gandhi.

AK requested Sonia Gandhi to invite Karunakaran to Delhi for reconciliation talks, and to stop all disciplinary action against his group. The anti-Karunakaran group had decided to remove M. P. Gangadharan from the position of Deputy Leader, of the Congress Parliamentary Party.

On 21 March, Karunakaran's second rally was taken out in Cochin and 13 MLAs appeared for the show. On 10 April, Murali was dismissed from the party for his anti-party activities. Only because of his age and seniority, was Karunakaran spared the guillotine, the AICC noted in a press release. In reply to the press release, the 'I' Group held another rally; this time in Trivandrum.

The Inevitable Split

On 1 May 2005, the Congress Party in Kerala split officially. Karunakaran formed a new party, and named it National Congress (Indira). Since the name resembled the Indian National Congress (Indira), they approached the Election Commission on the issue. The Karunakaran Group was asked to rename their party; they called it Democratic Indira Congress-Karunakaran (DIC-K). The anti-Karunakaran group dubbed it 'Dick'!

About a thousand followers of Karunakaran gathered in Trichur where their leader proclaimed the birth of his party. He had gone ceremonially about this naming business, in front of the Appan Thampuran Kovilakam. He thrice named the party in public in a ritualistic manner. Then he handed over to his son the party flag which bore the imprint of Indira Gandhi and the spinning wheel.

Nine Congress MLAs resigned from the party and turned 'DICK'. Earlier, the 'I' Group had claimed the support of 36 MLAs. When he formed his own party, Karunakaran resigned his Rajya Sabha seat. For more than three decades he had been steering the giant wheel of Congress politics in Kerala. Now he turned into the puny wheel of his own pigmy party.

The Two Standpoints

AK's stand was that there should be no disciplinary action against the Karunakaran Group; it would only weaken the Congress Party in Kerala. OC's stand was against any defiance of discipline; it would weaken the party entirely.

Balakrishnan Pillai and T. M. Jacob left the UDF. The former returned to the fold; the latter merged with DICK. The Congress High Command decided on 23 May 2005 that AK should contest the Rajya Sabha elections. This would mean several birds at one shot! Kerala Congress (M) and quite a few Congress leaders were clamouring for a seat. The High Command's decision proved a godsend. AK said that the dramatic and the unexpected had always played a lead role in his life. The Rajya Sabha seat was only another instance of the same.

The Elections

The occasional elections that he had to steer the Congress Party and the UDF through, were an ordeal to OC as CM. After the Congress split, he faced three such elections. On 2 June 2005, there were by-elections for Koothuparampu and Azheekodu Assembly constituencies; both had been the CPM's sitting seats and it saw victory in both the places, and with a wider margin to boot.

The Left Front performed tremendously well in the elections to the Local Administrative Bodies in September 2005. Five city corporations and 12 district panchayats went their way; so did most of the municipalities, block panchayats, and panchayats. DICK sided with the Left. In the by-election for Trivandrum Lok Sabha seat due to the demise of P. K. Vasudevan Nair of the CPI, UDF candidate V. S. Sivakumar was defeated by Panyan Raveedran, one of the Assistant Secretaries of the CPI. After the elections, Panyan rushed to Karunakaran's place to distribute ladoos. But a short while later, he and his fellows denied DICK's role in his victory.

The continuous defeats in the elections urged OC to give up his big projects for those that had a more popular appeal. Eggs for schoolchildren, three rupees for one kg rice for those below the poverty line, moratorium on agricultural loans, the Hungerless Kerala Project, and so on and so forth.

The Presidential Rise of Ramesh Chennithala

The split in the Congress Party, and the election defeats, led to the installation of a new KPCC President. On 24 June 2005 Ramesh Chennithala assumed that office. He led a 'Chaithanya Yatra' from Kasargode to Trivandrum, to inspire the party and the people.

The DICK Divides

After nine months, the DICK's dream of joining the LDF was over. Karunakaran and company sought to enter the UDF as an independent unit. OC opposed it tooth and nail. He was all alone in this battle. Some of the Congress leaders and major partners of the UDF backed the DICK plans. They mounted pressure on the Congress leadership in Delhi. After prolonged discussions, DICK entered the UDF, to fight the imminent Assembly elections. They were offered 19 seats. An agreement was signed between KPCC President Chennithala and DICK President Muraleedharan that DICK would merge with the Congress immediately after the elections. OC washed his hands clean off this deal. He knew that this was not going to be accepted by the people. The political climate had drastically changed in favour of the LDF. Though VS was denied a ticket initially, the public uproar forced the CPM Central leadership to rethink and he was given the Malampuzha seat in Palghat.

The elections to the Kerala Assembly were held in May 2006, in three phases. OC's physical movements were restricted after his slip in Davos and he was wary of the newly-imposed political alliance. A special vehicle was arranged for him to travel from place to place; he was the star campaigner. The UDF lost heavily. The LDF got 98 seats out of 140. DICK did not click; they could get just one seat. After the elections no one talked of the proposed Congress merger. OC was chosen to lead the Opposition. He and Chennithala worked in unison to revitalise the Congress Party and to win back the hearts of the people.

DICK later merged with the NCP, and Muraleedharan became its State President. Karunakaran left his son and rejoined the Congress. With his sad demise at the ripe old age of 93, on 23 December 2010, the Leader's (as Karunakaran was commonly called in the party) differences with the party were finally dissolved in the chill of his parting. Karunakaran is no more but his legacy lives on. He led the Congress in Kerala through many troublesome years and he was a known trouble-shooter glad to be of service to the party in the state and at the Centre. And Muraleedharan too was given a green signal to rejoin Congress on 15 February 2011 by the High Command ending his six years of political wilderness.

The NCP made another attempt to forge an alliance with the UDF in the 2009 Parliament elections, with no avail. Muraleedharan tasted bitter defeat in Wayanad. The UDF made a dramatic recovery, and won 16 out of 20 seats. The Congress fought the elections without any internal wrangling, after a long, long time. By-elections were held in Kannur, Ernakulam, and Alleppey Assembly constituencies in November 2009; the Congress won all three of them with comfortable margin.

The UDF made a remarkable stir in the elections to the Local Administrative Bodies in October 2010. They won eight district panchayats out of 14; 40 municipalities out of 60; and a majority of block panchayats and grama panchayats. The UDF bagged two corporations out of the five. The Congress and the UDF rose like the proverbial phoenix. They have now become a disciplined winning force. It happened since OC dared to risk even his own political future by keeping an iron fist in a velvet glove. Had he not taken a firm stand in 2005, would these victories have happened?

Within five years, all those who had left the Congress came back and were decently rehabilitated. Janatha Dal, Kerala Congress–J, Kerala Congress–B, Kerala Congress–Jacob, and Kerala Congress–Secular left the LDF and joined the UDF. The Indian National League left the LDF and the former CPM MPs, K. S. Manoj, S. Sivaraman, and A. P. Abdullakkutty, joined the Congress.

No CM till date has had to go through such turbulent and tumultuous days as OC has. In spite of it all he left a lasting imprint on the minds of the people as a towering CM.

OC completed 40 years in the assembly in September 2010. There was no celebration. He has been winning consecutively from Puthupally. He has been in Kerala's political arena, and on its fringes for more than five decades, first under the auspicious of the Kerala Studnets Union (KSU) and the Youth Congress, then as an INTUC leader, then as an MLA, Minister, UDF Convener, Opposition Leader, and Chief Minister.

Meeting the Prime Minister along with party MPs.

Receiving pleas and petitions from the masses.

Helping hands all round.

The common man's hero.

Visiting the sites illegally occupied by the vested interests in Munnar.

At Attukal Temple, Trivandrum.

With the Maharaja of Travancore next to a waxen recreation of OC himself.

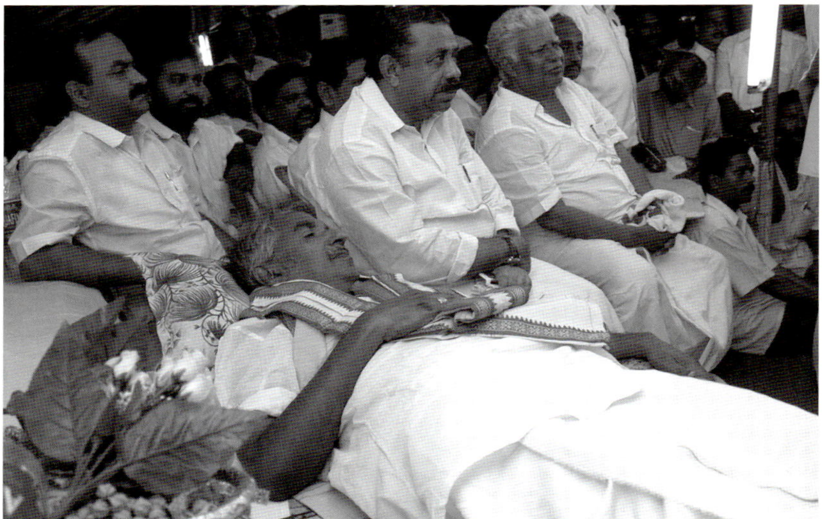

To fast, to strike, and not to yield.

In conversation with former President Dr A. P. J. Abdul Kalam.

By Gandhi! We have got to boycott.

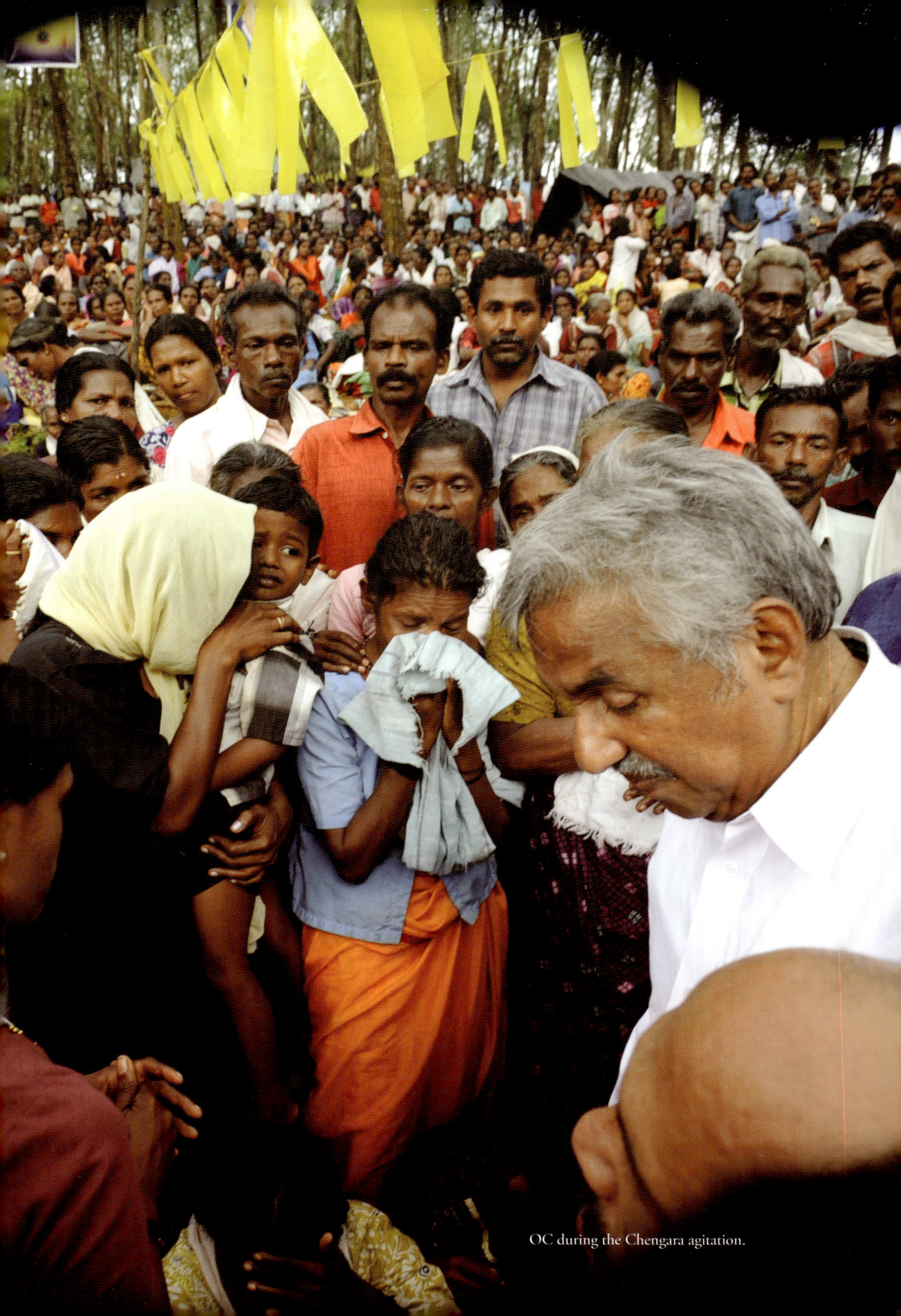

OC during the Chengara agitation.

A Youth Congress man.

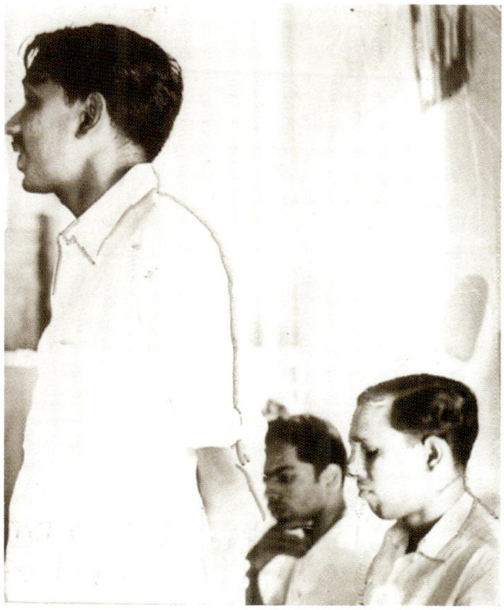

A KSU boy.

Ramesh Chennithala and OC in convivial company.

The charismatic crowd puller in action.

The rock of empathy.

Part Two

CHAPTER THREE

Foundations

Kerala Students Union

'Kunjunju' is a common pet name in Central Travancore. From 1970 onwards, one such Kunjunju of Puthupally, Kottayam, has been elected to the Assembly, without a break; he is Oommen Chandy. OC is now the apple of Puthupally's eye. He is the only one in the Congress Party in Kerala elected from the same constituency continuously for more than four decades now.

Old timers recall this lean Kunjunju's presence in Kerala politics from way back in 1957. That was a little after the Communist government of EMS Namboodiripad had come to power in the state. Scarcity of food supplies became severe and the government bought rice from other states. Charges of bribery and corruption were levelled against the government and the Congress set the Assembly ablaze. Congress leader T. O. Bava exposed the government's Andhra Rice Deal, quoting for proof the relevant bills and accounts.

The government had bought rice from two merchants, T. Sreemalu and P. Suryanarayanan. The first charge was that 1.66 lakhs was embezzled in the purchase of 5,000 tonness of rice. Later, a total of 16.5 lakhs were seen to have been misappropriated in the transaction. Bava traversed the length and breadth of the state to expose the Communist government's dirty deal. When his road show reached Puthupally, he was garlanded by young Kunjunju who went up the stage thus for the first time.

Kunjunju had started his political career at St George's High School, Puthupally. Rebellious days of the Kerala Liberation Struggle or the

Vimochana Samaram as it is commonly described, had enthralled him; he was then KSU Unit Secretary there. Close by was the V. J. Oommen Memorial UP School, started by his grandfather V. J. Oommen. Kunjunju's father, K. O. Chandy was its Manager and Headmaster. Kunjunju and friends marched to his father's school and demanded that classes be cancelled. Somebody rang the bell and the children came out of the classes. The Headmaster ran after the troublemakers. The fear of his caring made Kunjunju leap off the veranda where he landed in a pile of broken glasses. His feet were badly injured.

His father realised that V. J. Oommen's blood was flowing in young Oommen's veins. (V. J. Oommen had been a faithful follower of the State Congress and a member of the Sree Moolam People's Council. (The Sree Moolam Poeple's council or Sree Moolam Popular Assembly of Travancore was the first Popularly elected legislature in India) K. O. Chandy never again took up the cane against his son's political moves.

The *One Ana* Strike

The first EMS Government nationalised water transport in Kuttanad; all the boats were seized and brought under the Water Transport Corporation. Until then one ana (six paise) had been the ferry rate but it was raised to 10 paise. The students fought this move fiercely. It started in Alleppey, and spread to Kottayam and Ernakulam. The students clashed with the police in many places. M. K. Raveendran was their leader, the same man who later played a key role in both state and national politics as Vayalar Ravi.

The KSU was an infant. A few colleges had had a student union called Kerala Independent Students' Union. Another campus group had been the Students' Union. These two groups met and merged at the National Tutorial College housed in Thanu Iyer Boarding, Allepey, on 30 May 1957. Only a dozen odd students gathered there, and gave birth to the KSU (Kerala Students' Union) that day.

Vayalar Ravi was made General Secretary, and George Tharakan, its founder President. Later, Ravi became President of the KSU. A. C. Jose, was the third President. A. K. Antony was the fourth; and OC, the fifth. There was an unwritten rule that nobody was to be its President for more than two years. The KSU delivered a number of political leaders, chief ministers, central and state ministers, MPs, and MLAs to state politics.

When he was 17, OC became President of the *Malayala Manorama*'s 'Balajanasakyam'. the largest students organisation in Kerala then. The President's TA was to be paid by the Sakyam. Once, two of OC's TA bills were returned because the amount in the bill much lower than the actual cost. Another time on his way back from Cochin he was given a lift in a car. The travelling charge for the return journey was not entered in the bill. This time the bill was not encashed because it sought only half the expected expense! It was 8 kms from Puthupally to the *Manorama* office at Kottayam and the bus fare was four anas (25 paise). Often OC would walk the entire route, and save the whole amount.

A Dhoti Pulled!

OC travelled up and down the schools and colleges of the region trying to organise the KSU in Kottayam District. Once he went on this mission to St Thomas' College, Pala. The Kerala Students Congress (KSC) was strong in the campus there. Some of the KSC boys heckled him and his friend Thiruvanchoor Radhakrishnan. They forced the two on to the wall of the campus. Somebody from among the students tugged at their dhotis. The only way to escape public shame was to jump off the wall into the thick of the crowd which OC and TR did.

Hungry and Weary

There were times when Kunjunju did not have enough food because his lean purse could not afford it. He would skip the bus, and walk. He would sleep for the night at bus stations, and in the Congress Party offices. He would sit, through entire train journeys in the corridors of trains. The KSU leaders of his time had to, and did, put up with all kinds of such discomfort and inconvenience.

When OC was General Secretary of the KSU, he was running around, trying to strengthen the organisation in Central Travancore. A friend in Mavelikkara once promised to organise a meeting at his home for strengthening the KSU there. OC reached there in time. There was no sign of a meeting anywhere there. His friend was apologetic, and said that the KSU boys had gone for the Independence Day programme, and that he would mobilise them immediately. He went out and returned with a few. He introduced them as unit presidents of the KSU from the schools and colleges around. OC was garlanded by them and he gave them a long lecture. They parted happily.

After a few months OC reached Mavelikkara early in the morning, to meet his friend regarding a pressing matter. He went up to his house but his friend seemed to be asleep but there was light in the cowshed. Since OC was in a hurry, he went to the cowshed. There a boy was milking the cow. OC asked him a few questions and the boy answered them without showing his face. OC waited patiently until the boy got up after his milking. He was one of the KSU presidents who had attended his Mavelikkara meeting!

OC's friend had forgotten all about the meeting he had promised to convene. Only when he saw OC at his place that day, did he remember it. He was a very practical man. He went out and collected his own servants and some boys of the neighbourhood, and presented them before OC as KSU leaders.

Regarding his KSU days OC pointed out in an interview. 'We undertook social work amidst all kinds of inconvenience. The bus fare was often the biggest problem. We used to spend the night in the party office. We did everything according to the party line. There were many opportunities to work for the common good and those who served the people, were also recognised for their service. There are opportunities today, too. But recognition is slow or nil. For the group has triumphed over the party; the leader of the group is more important than the party leaders. The nomination system in the party has undone the leaders of a generation. In this, the senior leaders of the party, including myself, are to blame. It's a pity indeed!'

On the Campus

OC completed junior college (Pre-Degree) from CMS College, Kottayam; his under graduation (BA Economics) from St Berchmans' (SB) College, Changanacherry; and his law degree, LLB, from Law College, Ernakulam. Wherever he studied he led the students to react on social issues. During his first year at CMS, he initiated a strike for students' bus concession. That stirred up trouble and he was asked to bring his father to meet the principal. He told him to seek admission in some other college.

Pala K. M. Mathew, a prominent Congress leader from Pala, recommended OC to his relation, C. Z. Scaria, HOD, Economics, SB College, Changanacherry and OC joined SB. K. C. Joseph who later became an MLA was his classmate there. Those were days when SB College was allergic to strikes and student politics. Msgr Kalachery was Principal there. Instead of student unions, the principal would approve only of the Planning Forum, Social Service Forum, and similar bodies. The KSU decided to field P. T. Zachariah to the office of the Planning Forum Secretary. They quietly went about the election propaganda and Zachariah got elected.

Even during the heyday of his political activities, OC did not neglect his studies. When the exams drew near, he would concentrate on his studies for the preceding month. He had a remarkable memory, and passed all his exams creditably well.

The Golden Period of the KSU

OC got beaten up when he went to Kadaplamattom School, near Pala, to start a KSU unit there. The master who gave lead to it years later became his follower. At Kottayam and Quilon, OC was flogged for the same reason; those who then beat him were later glad to be led by him. Once he boarded a bus from Pala, to go to Ramapuram with the firebrand leader M. A. John. They had only four anas (25 paise) on them. The conductor asked for the fares. OC handed the four ana coin to him, and asked him to take them as far as that money could carry the two passengers. When they had to get off the bus, they walked the rest of the distance on foot.

One might as well say that the golden period of the KSU was 1967–69 when OC was its President and Kadannappally Ramachadnran and P. C. Chacko were the Secretaries. Those tumultuous days were marked by the strike against food storage; the Kasargode police firing that ended the lives of Sudhakaran Akithayi and Santharam Shenoy; the martyrdom of Murali at Thevara and other events.

Kerala had a coalition government of seven parties with EMS as the CM. EMS did not mind going forward with the rule of law mixed with strikes. His standpoint was unique. 'We would not abandon strikes because we rule the state. And we would not abandon the rule of the state for the sake of strikes.' No one has upheld such a policy of governance to date!

The main objection of the state government was that the centre was not providing Kerala with its necessary quota of rice. So they started a series of strikes against the central government. The KPCC fired back that Kerala government did not take adequate steps to collect and distribute the rice produced in the state. On the heels of this food crisis, came an endless procession of bundhs and strikes which nearly paralysed civil life in the State. The Opposition took the fight out on to the streets with the slogan: 'The Rule That Provides No Rice'. It was followed by the Ruling Front's official bundh! It was then that the police opened fire at the entry of Mallikarjuna Temple in Kasargode, killing Sudhakar Akithayi and Santharam Shenoy.

The KSU observed a Black Day, demanding judicial enquiry into the police firing. That started a course of collision between the police and the students.

The Storm!

On 30 September 1967, T. K. Murali (17), another KSU activist, died. He was a second year Pre-Degree student of Sacred Heart College, Thevara, Ernakulam. He had been among the students who had taken part in the march demanding a bus route to the college. He had slipped and fallen into a gutter, and had been beaten to death by the police. His father, N. P. Menon, charged the police with his murder while the government held that Murali had died of heart failure. The students erupted in fury. OC, President, KSU, demanded that an objective and impartial inquiry be conducted, and the perpetrators of the crime be punished. Until that was done, the students would go on an indefinite strike. The colleges were closed.

'Don't sow a wind and reap a storm!' OC's memorable words appeared on the front pages of newspapers the following morning. On 17 October, the students picketed the gate of Ernakulam District Collectorate, and were severely beaten up. OC's back was branded with baton fire. The next day, the police entered St Albert's College, and assaulted the students who were writing their exams, and the masters who were supervising them. The KSU leaders who prepared to stage a dharna in front of the CM's residence, were arrested and beaten up in the police stations.

EMS showered scorn on the students with an abusive comment, 'The lathi is no flute.' The state government which had led bundhs against the centre, had no right to advise the students to discipline, OC fired back. The KSU had come to stay as a force to be reckoned with in Kerala politics. The objections, remarks, and statements of its leaders made headlines in the newspapers. Its leaders became leading fighters in the vanguard of public life.

More strikes and struggles followed in defence of student rights. Some of their demands were for free school education, stopping detention; unifying the fee structure; allowing student representation in the University Senate; re-establishing the University Union and ending all capitation fees. The government had to give in to these demands. College Unions became training centres where students could learn the ABCs of democracy. The University Union would coordinate their activities.

The private college teachers struck work for 63 days demanding direct payment from the government. The KSU lent their wholehearted support to the cause. When the teachers' association appealed to the CM, EMS made a characteristic statement, 'I support you as a Marxist Party leader. But I can't as the Chief Minister of this State.' The private college managements took an unfavourable stand in the case; the teachers' strike came to nothing. The following year the college teachers gathered momentum for their demand when the strike for a unified fee structure stretched to 52 days.

Apart from strikes and agitations OC initiated several constructive programmes. One such initiative was paddy cultivation by students. 'A Bushel of Rice for Onam' was the slogan that emerged from the state camp of the KSU held at Kunnankulam, Trichur. The students after that camp went to a paddy field and worked there. Everybody appreciated it though nobody cared to continue it.

OC's torn Khadi shirt has been talked about from his KSU days. The rumour goes that he would tear it before he wore it when a new shirt was given him. In those days, the KSU leaders had just one or two pairs of clothing as most of them hailed from ordinary families. They would often borrow shirts and dhotis. OC would be given their discarded shirts by those who were closely acquainted with him. The torn khadar shirt became an insignia of the KSU as if it were its philosophical emblem!

Right from his KSU days, OC has not bothered about his clothing, food, or hairstyle. He would wear what he laid hands on. He would eat what he got. He would sleep where he could. He never really felt the need to comb his hair. Probably, he is too involved in his Karma to think of such mundane things.

The Youth Congress Times

When the KSU leaders outgrew their student leadership roles, they very often sat at the helm of the Youth Congress affairs. The Youth Congress gathered tremendous strength when A. C. George, M. A. John, and Vayalar Ravi took up its presidency. In 1968, it was A. K. Antony's turn to be president and Vayalar Ravi was elected as its National Secretary. When AK resigned, OC was appointed to that post.

AK's political tour of Kerala from Kasargode to Trivandrum and his Veluthully Lake Strike attracted wide attention. These were designed to protest against the Left Government's food Policy. 'No Rice; All Lies', was the slogan. There was an illegal move to portion off Veluthully Lake area to the followers of the Marxist Party. AK's strike was to prevent it. It stretched out for two and a half months.

The political scenario spelt anarchy in those days. In 1969, the Congress Party stood divided and then came the split. Four MLAs, under the leadership of K. Karunakaran, stood by Indira Gandhi while four others supported Morarji Desai's Syndicate Congress; T. O. Bava was its KPCC President. K. K. Viswanathan took over as the Indira Congress KPCC President. The youth wing of the Congress in Kerala lined up behind Indira Gandhi.

The Youth Congress' ways and attitudes gave the party a socialist, secular, and modern outlook in the state. They volunteered to lay roads in rural areas, dig wells and ponds, make latrines for dalits and tribals, and so on. They conducted a Tribal Development Seminar at Vattiyurkavu, Trivandrum. At the Cochin Convention of 1972, the Youth Congress resolved that educational institutions in the state should be nationalised, and that education should be a public sector enterprise.

The KSU and the Youth Congress facilitated the way for quite a few to the Assembly like A. K. Antony, A. C. Shanmukhadas, Kottara Gopalakrishnan, N. Ramakrishnan, Oommen Chandy. Others like

Vayalar Ravi, Kadannappally Ramachandran, A. C. George, V. M. Sudheeran, and K. P. Unnikrishnan became MPs.

Once OC and A. K. Saseendran had to travel by bus from Shornur to Ottappalam for a party function there. They had tea together and boarded a KSRTC bus. Everything was fine but then the bus broke down on the way. They could not wait for another KSRTC bus to take them to their destination. They would be too late for the meeting. So they decided to go by the next private bus (A privately owned bus as opposed to the state owned KSRTC). OC as an MLA had a bus pass but Saseendran did not have one. Neither of them had any money on them. They noticed a tailor dressed in khadar opening his shop. OC went up to him, introduced himself and borrowed one rupee, promising to pay it back. The tailor did not identify him, or believe him. One rupee was doled out as alms but that was enough for Saseendran's bus fare. After two months OC was back there; he repaid the amount, to the utter astonishment of the man in khadi.

Those were the days when most of the politicians sweated for service, not for mere greed. They worked without parliamentary desires. They were propelled by the zeal for reform. They fought corruption everywhere. They were led by a socialist outlook with modern ideas.

Once, after a KSU meeting at Palakkad, AK, Vayalar Ravi, Sudheeran, and OC were returning to Cochin. Since no other vehicle was available, they travelled in a lorry from Tamil Nadu. When the lorry reached outside Vadakkancherry, there was a blockade on the main road. The students waiting for their bus immediately recognised Sudheeran who was popular those days. He felt a bit embarrassed, and in order to smooth an embarrassing situation he reported that he was not alone but AK, Vayalar Ravi, and OC were there with him. The students were not ready to believe him and Sudheeran forced his colleagues to get down and paraded them before the students. OC wasn't there. He was fast asleep in the driver's cabin!

On 4 October 1970, C. Achutha Menon was sworn in as CM. Though the Congress had 32 seats, they did not join the Ministey for the first six months as 11 of the District Congress Committees and the Youth Congress had opposed the move. Karunakaran's group however, was ready to occupy the ruling benches. Achutha Menon called on Indira Gandhi, and urged the Congress to be with him. Youth Congress President OC who had represented the dissenting voice to the party boss, was asked, 'Should this Government continue?'

'Yes, it should,' was his answer.

'Then the Congress should join the ministry.' Indira Gandhi made it clear.

Karunakaran, Vakkom Purushothaman, K. T. George, K. G. Adiyodi, and Vella Eecharan were sworn in as Congress ministers.

In 1971, OC resigned as Youth Congress President. He concentrated on the labour unions and for this, he travelled far and wide in the State.

A Voice of Practical Politics

Phones and recommendations have always been OC's weakness. There are rumours that OC once wrote a recommendation letter to the US President. He did once send a letter of recommendation to Kim IL Sung, President of the Republic of Korea! This was at a time when a building for Kottayam DCC was being constructed. OC was Chairman of the Building Construction Committee which was going around for funds. Kim IL Sung's picture used to appear in many Malayalam newspapers in praise of the Korean leader. OC wrote him to finance an ad-page in the souvenir that they were going to bring out. He received a reply from the Korean Government. The ad had been permitted. OC would try even if the task seemed apparently impossible. He was, and is, a spokesman for practical politics.

Beauty Sleep on Newspaper Bundles!

In those days, OC's long journeys were on KSRTC buses. The midnight buses from Kottayam used to carry bundles of *Malayala Manorama* and *Deepika* dailies to Trivandrum and other distant places. Since he was a popular and frequent traveller, OC was allotted a place upon those bales for his undisturbed slumber. If it were by steamboat to Alleppey, a similar sleeper's slot awaited him on it. But for the chug-chug of the steamer, there was nocturnal silence everywhere. OC enjoyed those trips, gazing at the twinkling stars, and listening to the routine lullaby of the plying waters.

OCs frequent travels also meant that he could never get adequate rest. He once sustained a head injury in an accident in Manganam. Months passed but the injury remained raw. It became worse during one his nightly journeys by bus. It was cured only when he had to rest a year and a half later because chicken-pox laid him low.

A Leader of the Labourers

The labourers of those days were victims of all sorts of exploitation. OC started working among them. In 1970–77, he presided over some 40 unions. Besides these he was also President, INTUC, Kottayam District. The plywood industry flourished in Kottayam. OC started his trade union activities by uniting the men working in this area. He led a strike against the proprietors of Phoenix Plywood for having suspended a certain worker there. Which resulted in an important piece of legislation in Kerala, making suspension allowance legally binding. A great boon for hapless labourers! If a labourer was suspended for more than three months, he was to be paid half his wages. It would be three quarters of his pay if he was suspended upto six months. No one was to be suspended for more than six months. Otherwise the management would have to pay full wages.

In 1974, a labourer named Avarachy was hacked to death at Kottayam. His funeral procession was attended by well over 5,000 mourners. His death gave a greater impetus to the INTUC movement in the town. Those were days when labourers who stacked goods in lorries, were not regarded as workers at all neither by the porters themselves nor by the shopkeepers. OC united these men, and got their rights for them. Where the CITU alone had reigned supreme, the INTUC began to fly their flag high indeed.

Another strike was mounted against the MRF unit, Kottayam. The company had refused to give Christmas advance to the workers. Overnight, the MRF Worker's Union was registered. OC contacted the workers at the MRF, Madras, and confirmed that they would not turn traitors for their comrades and work extra to defeat the strike at Kottayam. S. Gopalan was the Labour Commissioner. There were occasions when OC had to continue negotiations past midnight, and into the early hours of the morning.

Butchers were the next to form a union of their own. Arrack shop workers had to depend on what their CITU bosses decreed; they had no legal system of rights recognised. OC's pioneering efforts saw to the legitimatisation of their rightful claims.

His extensive work among labourers of all kinds, was amply recognised when he was invited to take part in the International Labour Conference in Geneva, Switzerland. That was OC's first flight abroad, that too as a trade union leader. There is an interesting story about this foreign trip of his. The moment he left for Geneva, someone decided to raise funds on his account. The man went up to a businessman in the locality who had much affection for OC.

'Do you know that our OC is going to Switzerland?'

'Really!'

'There is a problem...He needs some money to purchase the ticket.'

Suddenly the businessman remembered a newspaper report.

'I read it in the paper the other day that OC has already left India.'

The man was taken aback. Yet he stood his ground.

'Oh, yes. It's true he left. He has to return, and you need a ticket for that, you know!'

OC's trade union activities were centred around the small INTUC office at Thirunakkara, Kottayam. Each morning he would go to the office, and get back home by night. On certain days he would stay overnight at the office itself. Once he was invited to preside over the meeting of the High Range Estate Plantation Employees Union at Elappara in Idukki district. When it was time to go, OC had no money for the journey. A close follower's wristwatch was pawned at a petrol station; with that money a jeep was hired for the trip. Food packets were distributed at the meeting. One extra packet became OC's supper on his return.

Toil and trouble conditioned the life of social workers in those days. Lack of funds was their main problem. OC was always with the workers, to stick posters, distribute notices, and so on. He was where his followers were. His leadership had flint and iron in it.

The Kanjiram Camp for agricultural workers conducted in 1975, drew much attention. It was attended by 500 labourers. The camp was inaugurated by Central Labour Minister Reghunath Reddy. The INTUC in Kerala spread its sphere of activity to the Railways, Electricity Board, Plantation Corporation, and other areas.

Union leader and Ex-Speaker of the Assembly, C. A. Kurian of the CPI, spoke of OC thus, 'Even when he occupied high offices Oommen Chandy remained a trade union leader and an organiser. On quite a few occasions, I have had to sort out labour disputes in association with him. My opinion of him has been shaped from this experience of mine.'

CHAPTER FOUR

OC–The Legislator

OC has been an MLA for more than four decades and won nine elections. His chief rival in this is K. R. Gauriamma who has won elections to the Kerala Assembly 11 times and twice before that to the Travancore-Cochin Assembly. K. M. Mani of the Kerala Congress has won 11 times from Pala, Kottayam.

From the very beginning OC made it a point to be accessible to the people at any time. Anybody could just walk in through his open door. During the 1970s, KPCC President K. K. Viswanathan happened to sleep in OC's MLA Quarter (Room No 38) when he was not there. Visitors who came to meet OC were surprised to see the door closed. One group pushed the door, and on finding KK in the cot they hurriedly disappeared. Then came another gang at midnight; they had been to a late-night cinema. KK send them packing, locked the door and fell asleep. Early in the morning visitors came from Puthupally. They knocked at the door, and called out OC's name. There was no response. One of them took a small stone and threw it in through the window. It hit the KPCC President! He rushed out, swearing never to sleep in OC's room again.

The Maiden Victory

The 1970 Assembly elections saw OC's maiden legislative journey to Trivandrum. Congress Leader K. M. Chandy had given him the party ticket merely for a nominal fight. He had observed, 'You might not get through at Puthupally. If you manage to the second place, we would count it as a victory.' It was a three-cornered contest there.

Chandy's apprehensions were out of place. OC defeated the sitting CPM MLA, E. M. George, by 7,911 votes. He was just 27 then. On 28 October 1970, OC made his maiden speech in the Assembly when discussions were on after the governor's speech on unemployment in Kerala. He observed, 'The severest problem that the youth today face, is unemployment. The administrators who have governed here so far, have gone about their business in a political manner, with temporary issues in sight; they have not sought to solve the problems of the young generation. This is the grave background of the present-day situation, with 15 lakh unemployed youth in the state.'

By 2005, the numbers of unemployed have reached thrice their 1970 number. Since he had intensely felt for their needs, he introduced unemployment wages when he became a minister. He has always come down heavily on the way biased criticism did the rounds in Kerala. People often take into account 'who' does things, not 'what' is done. This way the state has missed many a bus to integral development.

A Sudden Exit

Only once did OC make an abrupt exit from the Assembly and that too because of a sartorial blunder. It was years ago and he had just two sets of clothes. If there were more, somebody else was likely to take them away for their wear. The laundryman would take a soiled set for the washing, and bring the clean one for his daily wear. One day the man failed to turn up. OC had no clean clothes to go to the Assembly in. He went to the next room in the MLA Quarters. There he found the Kerala Congress Leader K. M. George's son. He borrowed his shirt and dhoti, and proceeded to the House. He at once became the cynosure of all eyes. His shirt was too large and too wide for his lean frame; it could well accommodate yet another like him. Laughter began to send ripples all around. OC struck a hasty retreat from the House.

Well-prepared Speeches

When OC rises to speak in the Assembly, even the half-asleep members and the slumberous alike would be alert; they had to be vigilant. He might hurl a bomb at any moment; none could be sure who was going to be blown up for he would come to the House only after doing thorough homework. He would be precise in his delivery; there might not flow any relentless eloquence or mellifluous inanity.

OC is of a rather grave disposition. His speeches hardly ever smack of rollicking fun or ludicrous farce. He cracks no jokes. Nor does he strive to supply titbits to find himself in the newspapers. Once, on being charged with corruption, he retorted that the accuser should beware he did not break his teeth on a stone. It drew thought-provoking laughter.

'Never does Oommen Chandy assay into political rhetoric when it is not opportune. When necessary, he does so but with restraint; his words speak volumes for his dignity and discretion,' observes journalist K. G. Parameswaran Nair.

'Even those Members, who habitually doze off in the Assembly, would be all ears when Oommen Chandy speaks there. He would not spend himself in igniting words. Whatever he had to say he would say, unto the last syllable. It would take quite some time before his listeners collected what was meant for whom,' journalist Joy Sasthampadickal avows.

OC would always be all attention to the accusations and barbed words of those against him. It redoubled when he occupied the CM's and the Opposition Leader's seat in the Assembly. Even the minute charges from the opponents would be taken down. Timely strategies would be devised to counter their inimical moves. OC was quite capable of such unpremeditated mastery of the moment.

'Political exchanges heat up the House; these often lead to quick challenges and sudden exits. The Assembly witnesses these sights and scenes quite frequently. On all such occasions, Oommen Chandy retains his customary cool, and conducts himself with mature composure; and that draws the house's attention.' This is former Speaker of the Assembly, M. Vijayakumar's remark.

An exemplary parliamentarian has to surmount several limitations. One, he has to speak effectively, and within the time limit. Two, he has to be objective. Three, he must always have done his homework. Four, he has to respond and retort at the spur of the moment. Five, he has to frame policy and design strategies, as and when necessary.

Plans and Operations

Many an act of legislation has been planned and piloted by him; these ought to be recorded for posterity in OC's credit. The most important among them was the Headload Workers' Law. It is, in fact, the workers' Magna Carta. As Labour Minister, OC spoke up for them on 9 August 1977. His bill sought to ensure welfare schemes for them, a forum to settle their labour problems, service conditions, and so on. Until then this neglected section of the community had no legal backing for their service. With uncertain wages and no permanence in their situation, they had to toil and sweat unto their last, ailing days. Now OC's bill brought them long overdue relief.

On the next day, OC introduced another bill. It was to protect temporary employees and substitutes from their exploitative masters. These two bills were passed by the Assembly after accommodating the views and suggestions of all who had supported and opposed them.

No Character Assassination at All!

Chief Minister, Opposition Leader, Minister, MLA–OC has donned several roles in the Assembly, and has always made his presence felt there by all and sundry. No matter how busy, he would not lose the seriousness of his mission in the House. Though calm by nature and meek in conduct, he lashes out when the occasion presses him to it. Time and again he has proved beyond doubt how one could oppose without violating parliamentary code and decorum.

OC would not speak without the backing of facts and figures. He has always observed current events, and collected the necessary details from his faithful followers far and near. His style is to approach a topic from all sides, and in different aspects.

'Even when he was deeply immersed in day-to-day political affairs, Oommen Chandy would do his homework related to every issue he has to deal with in the House. Another way of his was to present his view of the matter in an orderly, systematic manner.' So comments Therambil Ramakrishnan, former Speaker of the Assembly.

MLAs find ample opportunity to excel in the Assembly when they take part in the discussions during the question hour, budget session, legislation, unofficial bills, and so on. OC often comes up with new ideas and topics when he introduces submissions and emergency motions. These would include serious corruption charges if and when called for but never any biased observations, baseless accusations or character assassination. There is hardly anyone on either side of the floor, to vie with OC in bringing up current affairs of importance home to the House.

The Kakki Wood-felling Case

The only occasion when an accusing finger was raised against OC in the Assembly, was in connection with the Kakki wood-felling case. The accusation arose when he as Home Minister also held the Forests portfolio for 80 days. M. V. Raghavan of the CPM gave notice to the Speaker that the government had lost four crore rupees because of the extension of the contract for the removal of wood from the Kakki reservoir. When the tenders were invited to fell trees from the reservoir for a year, and the contract was granted, OC was not the minister concerned. The contract was renewed four times. OC had the additional charge of the ministry when the question of the contract came up for the fifth renewal. He stoutly refused all further extension.

He did not bow to the demand that a vigilance enquiry be conducted into the past four renewals of the contract. He said that it would be undemocratic and inappropriate to do so in a case where his predecessors had conducted themselves in good earnest. He would not be prejudiced against them, nor would he dare question their intentions.

Nevertheless he insisted on a judicial enquiry into his own conduct in this deal by a sitting judge. This was the last time that a sitting High Court judge made a judicial enquiry in Kerala. Thereafter the court never allowed a sitting judge for any such commission; the government had to seek the service of the retired judges. There are two reasons: one, judicial enquiry is often a farce; and two, the court is often short of judges. In OC's case, even those who accused him did not turn up to present their case before the judge. The commission did not even summon him to a session.

When personally accused, ministers frequently turn violently furious. They tend to forget that they are in the august presence of the most serious body of people in the state, and obviously ventilate their ireful vituperation in curses and damnations galore. OC has never lost his moral balance in the assembly. He has always responded to accusations and objections calmly, never spending himself in unravelling intemperate passion.

A Record

It was an unforgettable moment when the Prime Minister flew down to the state capital to honour the MLAs who had completed 25 years in the Assembly. OC was one among them. He is the only Congress MLA who has put in more than 40 years in the Assembly. There might not be many to compete with him in this regard even at the national level.

An able administrator or a model politician need not be a praiseworthy parliamentarian. OC has proved to be one. Nay, he is all three rolled into one. When he is on the ruling bench he could protect the cabinet as if within a magic circle. When he is seated with the Opposition he could hold the government at gunpoint. Such is his incisive understanding of legislative matters. His peak performance has always been on the floor of the Assembly.

'He does not draw the attention of the House because of his rhetoric or volleys of utterance. Nor does he cause discord there by a sudden leaping to his feet on any irritable spur of instinct, or by heckling anyone at will.' Thus goes former Speaker of the Assembly A. C. Jose's testimony.

OC does not take the House by storm. Similes and metaphors do not adorn his oratory. Yet everyone pricks their ears when he is up with his firm but graciously guarded words.

CHAPTER FIVE

The Hot Seat

An AICC meeting was held in Guwahati when the Emergency had reached its peak. AK, V. M. Sudheeran, and OC were also present there. Congress President T. K. Barua invited AK to speak and he spoke openly and courageously. AK pointed out that many criminal irregularities were being perpetrated in the shadow of the Emergency. His audience could hardly believe their ears. His speech hit the headlines on the following day.

Because of the Emergency, the Assembly elections due for September 1975 were postponed. On 3 October, the Achuta Menon Ministry completed five years, the first instance of its kind in Kerala. In March 1977, the general elections proved disastrous for Indira Gandhi and the Congress Party. In Kerala, the Congress and its allies were graced with great victory, 111 seats out of 140. OC doubled his earlier majority at Puthupally; he won over P. C. Cherian with a margin of 15,910 votes.

Karunakaran headed the new Ministry. OC was included in the cabinet as Labour Minister. He was 33 then. It was a most suitable reward for his selfless service in the labour world. But all things rosy soon came to an end. The verdict on Rajan's case came out. Karunakaran had perjured, according to the High Court of Kerala. He resigned on 25 April, 30 days after his swearing-in. KPCC President AK, a bachelor of 37, became the new CM, the youngest in his position in India. The 14-member Karunakaran Cabinet was retained. OC continued as Labour Minister.

Unemployment Wages

AK and OC alike had striven for the granting of consolation wages to the unemployed when they had presided over the destinies of the Youth Congress in the state. Now their ministry implemented the scheme. Concrete houses were built for the sordid hut and hovel dwellers of Chenkalchula, Trivandrum. (These were modified 28 years later when OC became CM again in the state.)

The Congress Splits

Meanwhile, mercury levels were changing drastically in the national politics. The Emergency turned out to be a stumbling block in the smooth run of the Congress Party. A split followed. Congress President Brahmanand Reddy suspended the Indira-supporter Devaraj Urs, CM of Karnataka. In protest, Indira Gandhi resigned from the Party's Working Committee. In January 1978, Indian National Congress-I was formed, with Indira Gandhi as President. Its repercussions were keenly felt in Kerala. Karunakaran and his followers stood by Indira; they were suspended from the official party. There were 18 MLAs with Karunakaran; the CPM had only 17. Karunakaran replaced CPM leader EMS as Opposition Leader. He was dubbed the 'Leader' in Kerala politics since then.

In November 1978, Indira Gandhi sought entry into the Lok Sabha from Chikamagalur, Karnataka. The central Congress leadership decided to support her there. In protest thereof, Antony resigned from the CM post. He later occupied the position of the KPCC President.

CPI leader P. K. Vasudevan Nair headed the new ministry. OC refused to continue in the cabinet. Owing to differences of opinion among the allies, the PKV Cabinet ceased to exist on 7 October 1979. C. H. Muhammed Koya headed the next. Later the Congress–U faction withdrew their support. A vain attempt was made to form yet another Ministry under K. M. Mani. But the governor dissolved the Assembly.

Anti-Left

The elections to the Sixth Assembly were round the corner. Some in the Congress–U faction lobbied for an alliance with the CPM. OC, Vayalar Ravi, G. S. Dharasingh, A. L. Jacob, and P. R. Francis opposed the move. The majority favoured the Left link and this alliance won the majority in the 1980 Assembly elections. E. K. Nayanar headed the ministry. From the Congress (U), P. C. Chacko, Aryadan Muhammed, Vakkom Purushothaman, and A. C. Shanmughadas were sworn in as Ministers. OC refused to be a Minister in the Left Cabinet.

In fact, he had not shown any interest even in contesting the elections. AK had insisted, and OC had consented. He defeated M. R. G. Panicker of the NDP with a margin of 13,659 votes. The MLAs wanted him to join the Ministry. AK had already promised Chacko a berth in the Cabinet. He was in a dilemma now. He should keep his word; that was the advice given by OC. The ministry survived for hardly 16 months. The Congress–U could not continue their liaison with the CPM for very long. AK formally ended that unlikely partnership by the end of October 1981.

The KPCC had taken that decision four days before the AICC meeting. AK could not attend it. It was OC who took part in it. He presented a paper there as to why they had to quit the alliance and the ministry; it was okayed by the AICC. Nayanar's resignation was accepted by Governor Jyoti Venkitachalam and the President's Rule was declared in the state.

Since there was no other alternative, AK sought to form an alliance with the Congress–I. OC wrote two letters to Sharad Pawar for his consent; the latter budged. He was anxious lest a three-cornered contest would ensue and sweep out the Congress (U) at the elections. Moreover, as the 'U' Group had been with the Left, their followers might flow into the 'I' Circle.

Six Congress MLAs, including P. C. Chacko and A. C. Shanmughadas, continued their support for the Left Front. AK, OC, and company now formed the Congress–A Group. Since OC had sharply criticised Sharad Pawar, he was the first to be suspended from Pawar's Congress.

A Home Minister for 80 Days

On 28 December 1981, Karunakaran headed the new ministry, with C. H. Muhammed Koya as Deputy CM. He had the support of the 'A' Group. OC was made Home Minister. He first sought to reform the state police. The khaki knickers and the pointed topee had rendered the constabulary look rather ridiculous. The force was now given a dignified costume, with pants and peak-cap.

In the Assembly, the ruling benches and the Opposition had an equal number of MLAs. The ministry was maintained by the casting vote of Speaker A. C. Jose. OC's duty was to bring all the MLAs together on the floor of the House for every session. Then Lonappan Nampadan of Kerala Congress–M crossed sides and the 80-day old Karunakaran Cabinet ended their reign. It was back to the President's Rule.

UDF Convener

The Assembly elections of 1982 fetched 77 seats for the UDF. OC won from Puthupally for the fourth time; he defeated Thomas Rajan, an Independent, by 15,983 votes.

Karunakaran again formed the 1982 ministry. Everybody expected OC to be sworn in as Home Minister as he had done a splendid job of that portfolio during his short tenure earlier. Vayalar Ravi stepped in, claiming seniority in the party. OC stepped back. Vayalar, Cyriac John, and K. P. Nurudheen were the 'A' Group members in the ministry. OC was elected as Leader of the Legislative Party of the Congress (A). In 1983 he was made UDF Convener.

The Merger

The rule together gradually led to the 'A' and 'I' combine. When

G. K. Mooppanar, General Secretary, AICC, landed in Trivandrum on 20 November 1982, he was received by OC. He gave OC a sweet thus signifying the sweet deal that was made. Later he affectionately embraced AK when the latter called on him at the Mascot Hotel.

The grand celebration of the formal unification took place at a mammoth meeting in Cochin on 13 December 1982 when Prime Minister Indira Gandhi flew down from Delhi for the historic event. In pursuance of the same, Karunakaran became Leader of the House and OC, Deputy Leader. This Karunakaran Cabinet ruled the State for full five years.

Those were eventful years. The SRP, RSP, and Janata (G) failed to remain as they had been; they further splintered into groups. R. Balakrishna Pillai resigned because of his 'Punjab Model' speech but re-entered the cabinet a year later. M. P. Gangadharan had to resign his ministerial berth because he gave his daughter in marriage before she had reached the age of consent. AK was appointed AICC Secretary. Indira Gandhi was assassinated on 31 October 1984. In the Lok Sabha elections that followed, the UDF in Kerala bagged 17 seats. In 1986, the CPM ostracised M. V. Raghavan and company for their 'alternative line' of action, urging the party to induct the Muslim League and Kerala Congress into the Left Front. MVR found refuge under the UDF umbrella.

By the end of 1985, Karunakaran felt the need for a cabinet reshuffle. After six months of protracted discussions on how to put a new 'face' on it, the Home portfolio was vacated by Vayalar Ravi; its reins were taken up by Karunakaran himself. OC expressed his dissatisfaction in this affair by resigning from his position as UDF Convener. In 1984, Vakkom resigned as Speaker because he was to run for the Lok Sabha. V. M. Sudheeran stepped into his shoes. He was against the government issuing too many ordinances instead of introducing them as bills in the Assembly. His ruling to that effect, led him on to a collision course with the government.

In 1987, the Left Front emerged victorious. Nayanar became CM for the second time. OC defeated V. N. Vasavan (CPM) by a margin of 9,164 votes. The Left miscalculated, and failed to repeat their Assembly victory in 1991. Rajiv Gandhi's tragic death had sent sentimental waves across the state and the UDF found their way back with Karunakaran as CM for the fourth time. OC defeated Vasavan again, now by a margin of 13,811 votes. This time around he was made Finance Minister.

Finance Minister

OC drew large crowds into his ministerial office. He was most seen amidst a multitude of visitors. Reputed journalist K. R. Chummar nicknamed his office a 'Maveli Store'. OC's visitors would queue up, or crowd together there, as if they were shopping at a public outlet.

OC was second in command in the cabinet though he was absolutely the same old Oommen Chandy. Once, he was to hoist the national flag at Pathanamthitta on Republic Day. He was home at Puthupally. When he woke up in the morning, he found that he had no clean shirts. The one he had on was rather soiled. He saw a local leader arrive there dressed in immaculate khadar. OC asked him to get into the State Car. The poor man had no idea of the minister's design. On the way OC asked him to give him that shirt. The Finance Minister attended the Republic Day celebrations that morning in a borrowed shirt. On his way back, he returned it to its original owner.

The Finance Minister had trouble with his treasury; it did not have sufficient funds to run the state. The overdraft from the Reserve Bank alone kept the clock ticking. OC's fiscal management enabled Kerala to correct the slide in three years.

When the ministry had completed a year, Karunakaran met with a road accident and a political crisis ensued. OC was made the leader of the UDF in the Assembly. However, he was sidelined and Power Minister C.

V. Padmarajan was given the CM's duties. Revisionists in the Congress emerged while Karunakaran was confined to his bed.

The Budget Speeches

OC's speech on 19 July 1991, introducing his maiden budget as Finance Minister, caught the ears of the House, and the columns of the papers. That budget was presented amidst many limitations, in the middle of the financial year, and with a deficit of 55.11 crore rupees. OC had realised that unemployment was the worst problem that Kerala faced. He took a series of steps to ease the situation. He pinpointed four policies to revitalise the sources of production; these had to do with agriculture, industry, energy, and water management. His second budget speech was delivered on 20 March 1992. It declared a number of ways of curtailing the expenses, and urged the government and the common man to observe 1992 as a Thrift Year. New offices would not be started. New vehicles would not be bought. Government's telephone bills would be reduced to half. Deputation allowances of the government staff would be stopped. The budget deficit shrank to 26.64 crore rupees. It was presented when the state was passing through a severe economic crisis. OC concluded his speech on a hopeful note, quoting from Shelley's *Ode to the West Wind*: 'If winter comes, can spring be far behind?'

On 12 March 1993, he presented his third budget. It was a time when the world economy was being refashioned by globalisation and liberalisation. OC was subject to the influence of these ideas. New measures to check the expenses were pursued. Accordingly, evening colleges were stopped; the offices and staff of completed projects were abolished and excess employees were deployed.

The Palm Oil Controversy

The Palm Oil Controversy reared its stormy head in Kerala politics during this period. T. H. Mustafa held the Food and Civil

Supplies portfolio. The *Kerala Kaumudi* had scooped out the CAG report on the import of palm oil before the Assembly met. The Accountant General then was son-in-law to RSP leader Baby John, the 'Kerala Kissinger'.

It was a time when OC had serious political differences with Karunakaran, and three months after he had resigned from his ministerial office. Yet he spoke strongly in defence of the CM regarding the palm oil deal. He proved in the Assembly how the government had, in fact, stood to gain 8.5 crores through the import.

He concluded his speech quoting from EMS's words used in defence of himself when he had been accused of corruption in the Andhra Rice Deal. 'Our Prime Minister has for long been fed up with the red tapism and delays of routine administration particularly. The government is determined to take all possible steps to remove this delay and get things done quickly. The government therefore regretfully expresses its inability to accept the commission's findings in this respect.'

Ravi's Victory

On 31 January 1992, Vayalar Ravi defeated AK by 18 votes, and took over as President, KPCC. That same year AK was made member of the Congress Working Committee. It was possible after a war of votes in which OC played a key role, to ensure his friend's safe passage to Delhi. On 17 January 1993, Antony was sworn in as a central minister.

OC's Resignation

OC's withdrawal from the ministry had to do with the controversy that raged in the Congress regarding the Rajya Sabha elections in the state. That happened on 16 June 1994. It was on account of M. A. Kuttappan, of 'A' Group, being denied a seat, the same having been given to Vayalar Ravi. AICC General Secretary Ahmed Patel had called OC to inform him that Kuttappan would have to withdraw his nomination. The 'A' Group gathered at Thycaud House, the official residence of Forests Minister K. P. Viswanathan, to discuss their future course of action; 16 MLAs took part in it. After their deliberations Kuttappan withdrew his nomination, and OC decided to resign from the cabinet.

Accompanied by K. C. Joseph and Palode Ravi, OC reached his office, and went through the two remaining files. The last file that he affixed his signature to was for the purchase of a bus for Kottayam Engineering College. He called up his PS, M. Narayana Pillai, and Finance Secretary M. Mohankumar, and told them he was quitting the cabinet. Officers and party workers filled the place. The telephone kept ringing; OC's few words were, 'Yes, it is true, There's no other way, Sorry, I've got to go.'

OC heard that Karunakaran had arrived in the CM's office at 3.15 pm. He started out; at his heels was a fleet of photographers and reporters. At 3.20 pm, OC tendered his resignation to Karunakaran. It read:'Dear Chief Minister, I'm resigning from your ministry. Thanks for the cooperation extended to me so far.'

Later OC spoke to the press. 'A K Antony had allowed himself too many adjustments and compromises for the sake of effecting and maintaining unity in the Congress Party. Even a year after the unification, one group has not yet been able to imbibe the spirit of unity.'

It was after ringing up AK in Delhi that OC handed over his resignation. AK was choked with emotion. He knew for sure that OC must have been deeply hurt; otherwise he would not have resorted to resignation.

Karunakaran's Resignation

OC's resignation resulted in commotion in Congress politics in Kerala. Twenty MLAs signed a memorandum, urging the High Command to unseat Karunakaran from the CM's chair. Forests Minister K. P. Viswanathan, who had been one of the signatories, was asked to resign by the CM. Viswanathan did not pay heed to it. The ISRO espionage case hastened Karunakaran's resignation.

The Kerala Government found it difficult to sail smoothly. The Opposition-led strike against the self-financing colleges, turned violent. When the DYFI gheraoed Co-operation Minister M. V. Raghavan at Koothuparampu, the police opened fire and five were shot dead on the spot. The coalition parties also demanded Karunakaran's resignation and Prime Minister Narasimha Rao had no other options left before him. On 16 March 1995, nine months after OC's resignation, Karunakaran had to follow suit.

The MLAs and the Congress leadership supported AK who had resigned from the central ministry on 14 December 1994 because his name had been dragged into the sugar import controversy. AK was sworn in as Kerala CM. V. M. Sudheeran joined the cabinet in lieu of K. P. Viswanathan. OC stayed away from the ministerial circle.

Karunakaran later became a member of the Rajya Sabha, and was inducted into the Central Cabinet. In the May by-election that followed, AK emerged victorious from Thirurangady, defeating Left candidate N. A. Karim.

In April 1996 the UDF had to face defeat in the Assembly elections. AK now became the Opposition Leader. OC defeated Reji Zachariah of the CPM with a margin of 10,155 votes. It was his seventh consecutive win at Puthupally. In 2001, OC defeated Cherian Philip by 12,575 votes. In 2006, his margin shot up to 19,863. Sindhu Joy of the CPM was his rival that time.

The rest is history.

Part Three

CHAPTER SIX

Home Is Where The Heart Is

There are two records that should be entered in Oommen Chandy's name. The first for the largest number of journeys a Kerala politician has undertaken and the second for the largest number of visits to wedding feasts and funerals. OC can rightfully claim this award because of his innumerable travels in Puthupally and visits to people there.

He has brought much development to his village. Puthupally has, in turn, made him a political star. He would not choose to lose his hold there. OC now divides his time between Puthupally in Kottayam District, and 'Puthupally House' in Trivandrum.

A Miniature World

Puthupally is his world. It is a provincial town with a little too much of the rustic and rural about it. It is eight kms east of Kottayam town. The St George's Church there is centuries-old and Puthupally is centred round it. On the feast day of the saint, thousands of pilgrims flock to church. Saraswathi Temple, Panachikad, is also in Puthupally constituency. On the day of Vijayadasami, thousands of children are brought to the temple, also called 'southern Mookambika' for initiation into the world of learning. Apart from these, it is only after OC attained political stardom that Puthupally began to attract greater attention.

When OC reaches his native place he becomes Kunjunju, meaning a small infant. To the folks in Puthupally, he is still a 'baby'. His personal relations there rise above caste, creed, and party considerations. He personally knows almost everyone and every house there. OC is too busy, at times, to visit a house when a wedding is celebrated there. Nevertheless he would drop in even if it was late in the night, and the lights were out. He makes it a point to wish the newlyweds the very best in life.

OC once attended the wedding of an ordinary Congress worker. The man was very excited at the arrival of his leader. The host personally served food for the VIP. He was so thrilled that, instead of sambhar, he poured squash in OC's plate. OC found his rice unpalatable but he quietly ate it just to humour his host.

The man later inquired, 'How was the meal?'

'Oh, it was sweet indeed!', OC replied.

He would not leave out a house in Puthuppally where someone passed away. No matter whether the burial or cremation was over or not, OC would pay a visit there. There has been many an occasion when he sped to Puthupally, 150 kms away, for such a visit, and returned to Trivandrum at the same speed. Usually these trips are taken by train at night to save money and time. He would leave by Kannur Express at 8.30 pm and reach Puthupally by midnight. In the next two hours he would make quick visits and return by the Kannur–Trivandrum Express at 2 am and reach the city early in the morning.

Once he was speaking at the anniversary of a school in his home town when he heard that a former teacher of that school had died. It then turned out to be a memorial meeting. Afterwards OC proceeded to the dead man's place. But before he could reach there, he was informed that the teacher had not died; he was only seriously ill and hospitalised.

It was indeed an embarrassment but OC had to get over it. He continued with his visits for the day and at the end of it when he was heading home for a quiet slumber, an acquaintance of his finally reported:

'Sir, we've managed to pull it through this time.'

'What?'

'That teacher has indeed passed away!'

Once OC arrives at Puthupally, the place has a festive air. Crowds follow him everywhere, at home, in the church, on the road. The people would even play tricks merely to have him visit their home.

One Congressman, tried time after time, to take OC home for a visit. Each time OC would say, 'When there is an appropriate occasion, surely I will visit you.'

One day the man rang up OC and reported that his mother was very ill, and that her last wish was to see 'Kunjunju'. Of course, OC was moved, and proceeded to his place though he was very busy with by-election activities in Ernakulam Lok Sabha constituency. When they alighted from the car, OC and company had to walk some distance. As they neared the house, OC felt that there was something fishy. There was not a sign of mourning anywhere and the desperately ill mother was sweeping the courtyard!

The man was furious with his mother. 'I had told you, Mother, to lie down till OC came and you are standing here with a broom.'

'I lay down for a long time. Then I thought Kunjunju would not turn up at all.' She defended herself.

The Durbar

Almost every Sunday that OC has been home in Puthupally for the past many, many years a durbar follows after Holy Mass in the morning. His dwelling is not that large. The people assemble in the yard, defying the scorching sun and the sweltering weather. Wherever he is in India, OC would try to be at Puthupally on every Sunday. After the accident at Davos, Switzerland, a few such durbars were cancelled.

In the Andhra Assembly elections of 1985, OC had the charge of the Naxal-ridden Nizambad, Karim Nagar, and Adilabad. He would set out at five in the morning to meet the people in these districts, and decide on the Congress candidates for these regions. Meanwhile the People's War Group declared a bundh. OC could not allow himself to be tied down to a hotel. With some companions he headed for Adilabad by taxi, 150 kms away from Nizambad, early in the morning. On the way, they witnessed battered vehicles undone by the mines that the Naxalites had planted minutes before their arrival. When they reached the Adilabad MP's house, the people there could hardly believe their eyes.

That journey had to be undertaken that very day. Otherwise OC could not return to Puthupally for his Sunday durbar. He had to defy the bundh and he did. All for Puthupally!

Once a humorist quipped on how OC winds up his business with his audience at Karot Vallakkalil House, Puthupally. 'OC would ask if anyone else was there to see him. It was quite like the question voiced everyday at Vaikom Temple whether anyone else was there to be fed.'

OC would not feel hunger or exhaustion when surrounded by a crowd. He would encounter the 100th person as enthusiastically as he welcomed the first one. Only then would he proceed to the next programme. He would hear out everyone's complaint or request as they stood around him. There was no queuing up or feeding data into the computer for the purpose. OC would turn his head this way and that, to listen to everyone, as if he were in a confessional! The answers and the solutions would be dispensed with, right there and then.

His aides would be around to take care of the redressals, arrange a telephone call, to write out a letter or anything else he wanted them to do. OC always has his say in everything. Those who go to him, have many different wants and demands. A sizeable number of those who flock together at his Sunday gatherings, are the ailing, suffering from common cold to incurable cancer. He would not disappoint anyone of them, the ones with simple ailments or the terminally ill.

His companions at Puthupally vouch, 'He would hardly have any proper food or rest. Often he fends for himself on a few slices of bread or a banana that we would fetch for him. He is no finicky gourmet, for that matter.'

When a vehicle is ready for him to go somewhere, it is with much ado that he finds a place in it. His companions and followers crowd and squeeze in before him and he would not say no to them. Such inconvenience does not annoy him. There were occasions when he would have to wait outside the vehicle until someone graciously vacated his seat for Kunjunju to travel in. He would, of course, have to put up with much jolting and jostling on his journey by car. Once he could not get into his car at all. Nobody was willing to vacate their seat; and he did not want to embarrass anyone, either. He saw a scooter nearby and opted for a pillion ride on it.

The people of Puthupally have a proprietorial claim on their Kunjunju. They step into his house with such loving freedom. At times they would even unleash their temper on him; he would show them his other smiling check. Once, OC reached home very late at around two in the morning. There was somebody waiting for him. While he was explaining his problem, OC started dozing. The man became furious, and he pinched him. OC jumped out of his chair.

There is no other politician in Kerala who is so thoroughly deprived of his privacy. At Puthupally, OC is common property. He would seem to welcome everyone's intrusion. Even if it were into his bathroom! To say that, would not be too hyperbolic either, for he is father, son, and brother to the whole of Puthupally.

Never has the village witnessed a day like the one when their Kunjunju resigned as Finance Minister and reached Puthupally. That night, hardly a house there allowed the lamp or candle to burn out. OC was garlanded and welcomed at every nook and corner of his constituency. Endless gatherings and meetings went on till the wee hours. These were preceded by the meeting at Kottayam where hundreds of vehicles and thousands of people assembled. A similar gathering was witnessed only when P. T. Chacko had resigned as Home Minister, and was hosted a heroic welcome there.

Puthupally's Own CM!

Puthupally has made him who he is and he has seen to the growth of Puthuppally. It is OC who brought all kinds of institutions there, from the anganvadi to the engineering college. Puthupally could not, and did not, sleep for riotous jubilation on 31 August 2004 when her Kunjunju occupied the chair of Chief Minister, Kerala. By midnight OC bade good night to the celebrations in the capital city, and sped with his family to Puthupally.. He was heartily welcomed by his mother Baby, and by his countless followers. Sweets were distributed and then they went to church.

On one occasion the CM reached home at eight at night. Everyone had gone to church. It was the Feast of St George. His personal staff had set out from Trivandrum with a number of files; they would take two more hours to reach Puthupally. Without any air of Chief Minister of the State, OC walked alone to Puthupally Junction. At the junction, a few people gathered around him. Soon it grew into a large crowd.

Once, a certain organisation decided to stage a protest march to his house at Puthupally. He waited for their arrival but they were getting late. He went out of his way to meet them. The men were just getting ready to start the procession from the next junction. Someone was ventilating his deadly fury against the Chief Minister over the loudspeakers. Voila, the Chief Minister appeared before him in the crowd. Quite a few hailed him, shouting slogans on his behalf. In no time the speaker turned the tables upon himself, and started a series of rhetorical somersaults in defence and adulation of OC.

OC's Genealogy

OC's Puthupally connection began with his paternal grandmother. A century ago, V. J. Oommen (of Vallakkalil, Mannar) married Achamma (of Karot family, Puthupally). He was a State Congress worker, and a member of the Travancore Sree Moolam People's Council, 1934–38. His family had been rich and influential but then their coir business failed.

There were only two girl children in the Karot family. Oommen married the younger sister and he took up residence at Puthupally. The new family came to be called Karot Vallakkalil. Oommen started a school near his house. He fathered five children. K. O. Chandy was the eldest of them. He changed the school's name to V. J. Oommen Memorial School; he became its Manager and Headmaster. Chandy married Baby, of Oruvattythara, Kumarakom, Kottayam. It was at Baby's home that OC was born on 31 October 1943.

Chandy had three children. The eldest is Valsamma; she married and settled down near her father's place. OC is the second. The last-born is Alex; he now stays in the family residence. He is now manager of the school as well. It used to be a girls' only school. In those days, the male children of managers and teachers were permitted to study in girls' schools. OC and Alex felt embarrassed to sit beside the girls; so they pursued their upper primary studies at St George's Government High School, Puthupally.

The three children formed fine company. Kunjunju was the lamb of the trio; Alex was the naughty lad. When Kunjunju was in the third standard and Alex in the first an incident happened during Sunday School. While the Mass was being celebrated, Alex rang the church bell. During the Sunday school that followed, the parish priest identified the culprit, and got ready to cane him. Alex fled the classroom, and took shelter in Kunjunju's class. The priest came after him. Kunjunju admitted Alex's fault as his own, and got caned for his brother's sake. Indeed, OC was marked out for a selfless line of life right from his tender years; the only difference is that his sphere of activity has extended today beyond his family and his little town.

There are quite a few leaders who have made their constituency their real home. At Puthupally, there is no difference between the MLA's house and his constituency. That is why OC named his residence at Jagathy, Trivandrum, as 'Puthupally House'. It is obviously more than a political symbol; there is an overriding personal emotion that sanctions and sanctifies the nomenclature.

Little wonder, as Chief Minister, OC did not move into the official Cliff House; he continued to reside at Puthupally House itself, the domestic inconvenience notwithstanding. Nor did he, as Opposition Leader, shift his family to the Cantonment House, the official residence of the Leader of the Opposition. 'Puthupally House' means much more to him than any palatial residence that the state could honour him with.

CHAPTER SEVEN

His Fair Lady

For long, OC had not thought of marriage. He had decided to be married to social work and a political career. Even his younger brother got married before he did. His relatives sought relentlessly to yoke him in holy matrimony. When finally cornered, OC drew up a few conditions. He would marry the first woman whose proposal came, he would not go to a woman's place for 'bride-inspection' and he would not take any dowry.

His brother-in-law P. J. Mathew arranged the whole affair. OC was taken to his aunt's place at Pallam, near Kottayam, for a glimpse of the girl. The two were too nervous for a long conversation. Mariamma, affectionately called Bava, was working as a clerk with Canara bank. OC asked her about the bank employees' union. She answered the question. There were no other words exchanged. In five minutes the interview and the courtship were over. OC had seen her photo earlier, and had fallen for her slim frame. Her family had at first rejected this proposal because they thought he was 39. The clarification came; he was only 33.

Mariamma was a little apprehensive about a politician-husband. She prayed hard. If the man were of the corrupt kind, the proposal would surely fall through. The truth about OC was most heartening for any bride. He not only who hailed from a famous Syrian Christian family but also had a promising political career. He had already made his mark in Kerala politics and was known as incorruptible.

Mariamma came from a similar Syrian Christian background. She was born into the Kuzhithallil family of Karuvatta in Kuttanad; daughter of Abraham and Achamma. Her grandfather M. Mathew of Kuzhithallil,

Kottayam, was the first among Syrian Christians to be elevated to the rank of a Munsif and when he was Munsif of Harippad, his family settled at Karuvatta.

The Marriage of a Minister

The proposal was okayed but the marriage had to be postponed for the 1977 Assembly elections came up. OC's victory must have been most celebrated by Mariamma. She confesses she never had as much joy even when her man was made chief minister. OC was inducted into the ministry but he was too busy to think of wedlock. The endless postponement sent tremors in the bride's family. The engagement took place in the absence of the groom but with the consent of the two families. The engaged couple occasionally spoke to each other over the phone but for her lengthy letters she would only receive brief replies.

Five months after the betrothal, the marriage took place at Mar Kuriakose Dayara, Pampady, on 30 May 1977. The solemn occasion was not accompanied by any fanfare. There was no pomp and splendour as might be expected of a ministerial nuptial. A few dailies carried an announcement regarding the same. Nobody was invited to the wedding and no wedding feast was prepared. There was not even a glass of lemonade for a parched throat. The bride's party had to attend feast on their own. The groom had set aside all programmes for the day with the 'excuse' that he had to go to a wedding at Puthupally!

Though no one was invited to it, many people came to attend the ceremony. Mariamma began to get used to the crowds from that day onwards. After the wedding, the pair proceeded to the bride's place as custom demanded. But they did not stay there for the night.Her mother placed Bava's hand in Kunjunju's, and bade them farewell. Mariamma did not feel the full impact of it then. She could do so only when her own daughter Maria set out from her place with her husband after their wedding. That was heart-rending for her. The newlyweds reached Trivandrum at one in the morning; they settled at OC's official residence, the 'Prasanth'. It was much later that they moved into their own 'Puthupally House' at Jagathy.

Bava queried if she might call him 'Achayan' which is a customary name that wives call their husbands in the Christian tradition. OC said, no. So she shortened 'Kunjunju', and made her own petname–'Kunju'. Since then OC has been Bava's only Kunju.

Bava's one complaint is that her Kunju is not home as often as he should be. He comes home late in the night and at times leaves before anyone knows he was there. Once, when he was opposition leader, OC reached home from Ernakulam around 8 at night. There was nobody at home except the gunman. OC was very hungry; there were nothing edible at home. The gunman asked if he needed something to eat. OC was reluctant to use the gunman on kitchen duty. The man provided OC some hot water and tea. It actually intensified the hunger. OC looked around and found a few small rotten bananas kept for the parrot. These sufficed him for the supper.

Mariamma was on leave from the bank immediately after the marriage, and was eager to get transferred to Trivandrum. Kunju would not hear of it. There would be remarks passed on all around if the transfer materialised so soon as that, he said.

Kunju and Bava have three children: Maria, Achu, and Chandy. When they were born, their dad was out of station on each occasion. At the eldest's birth, OC was away accompanying Sushma Swaraj, Housing Minister, Haryana, who was in Kerala to study the Chenkalchoola Housing Project in Trivandrum. When Achu was born, her father was attending the KPCC Executive meeting at Ernakulam. When the third was delivered at Cosmo Hospital, Trivandrum, at two in the morning, OC was fast asleep at home.

Karot Vallakkalil at Puthupally, 'Puthupally House' at Jagathy, Room

No.38 at the MLA Hostel, (Chief) Minister's office, Opposition Leader's place, are all inn-like dwellings to him. Privacy has always been a rarity in his life. Bava has had to rather impatiently to put up with it.

As a matter of fact, OC hates loneliness. He fears to spend time in an ICU for no hospital would allow bystanders there. After the accident at Davos, he was taken to an ICU for an emergency operation. When he regained his consciousness he asked for a meeting with those who accompanied him. Thereupon he was removed to a private room.

A Small Matter

Bava has but one small demand. When OC is home he should be with the family, exclusively for at least half an hour. Ten minutes for family prayers, 15 minutes for food, and five minutes for some conversation! It does not seem an impossible demand. Not so with OC! As he lifts the food to his lips, his phone might ring and come between his mouth and the morsel. The telephone conversation steals into his family time as well. The phone, to be sure, is an extended limb to him.

Though the phone is his weakness, OC has no mobile of his own. As CM, the government allowed him the use of a cell phone. OC would not use it. Instead he would borrow one of the mobiles of those of his retinue or of anyone of his gunmen's. When the Assembly reckons the ministers' mobile expenses, OC's as CM would be a mere zero. When he was Finance Minister he discontinued the STD facility in his office, and set a model for all Ministers.

For a long time now OC has had no barber to do his hair-cutting. His wife Mariamma, does it for him, while he is asleep, or going through the newspapers! OC is too busy to pay attention to his hairstyle. Mariamma got tired of her husband's dishevelled and overgrown hair that she took to cutting it herself and OC found it convenient, too. Thrift, indeed! Even when he was Chief Minister, Bava was his barber.

Bava in *Set Mundu*

Kunju loves to see his Bava in the typical Keralite *'set mundu'*, with a bindi on her forehead and her eyebrows done in artful black. Once she wore jasmine in her hair, and travelled with her husband on the Amrita Express. But that was food for cheap gossip in some press, and occasion for silly controversy. Kunju is fond of Bava's long hair. When she contracted sinusitis Bava bobbed her hair. Kunju came home, and was quizzed by the children regarding the change in their mum's appearance. He blinked in innocent ignorance. Head over heels in politics, OC has had little time for such romantic sentiments.

Bava was put to the test when Kunju was back home after his Davos accident and his mother was hospitalised after a fall. OC expressed his deep-felt concern as Bava was running around doing everything. Very rarely does he openly express appreciation. Love is not to be buried within a brimming heart; it is to be expressed as and when possible. That is the heart of the matter according to Bava.

In 1983, the MLAs got a chance to visit America. They were not supposed to take their spouses along. But OC declared that he would not go without his wife. Finally, the permission was granted. Since both of them together were not provided hotel accommodation, they stayed with friends and relatives in the States.

During their early days of married life, Bava would insist on going to the cinema together. But they could not have their time solely to themselves. As Minister, OC had to be accompanied by his gunman. Once, when the film started, someone was spotted in the next seat; one who seemed far from friendly. Bava was so afraid that the gunman was asked to be seated by the minister. After that incident, the couple stopped going to the cinema together. That was the end of OC's film-seeing as well. When Mohanlal, the Malayalam tinsel icon completed 25 years, in filmdom, he held an interview with OC. He asked him what was the latest film that he had seen. OC replied*Manjil Virinja Pookal* (The flowers that bollmed in the snow). That, incidentally, was Lal's first film.

After their marriage OC told Bava three things. One, half the image of a politician was his wife. Two, Bava should keep her footwear outside when visiting a house and three, instead of remaining in the drawing room she should go in and socialise with the people they were calling on. Bava has since then conducted herself accordingly.

Kunju has not however, responded to Bava's requests regarding his dishevelled hair, careless attire and ceaseless travels. Dyeing his hair would surely make him look 10 years younger. OC hardly shares his troubles and problems with anyone. It tells upon his health, observes his anxious wife.

After years of persuasion Bava has brought about some slight changes in him. Every Sunday he goes to church and only after that does the Puthupally Durbar begin. On rising from bed, he prays for a few minutes. Bava spends quite some time on spiritual affairs, and for social welfare activities.

When AK Got Married

Mariamma played cupid for A. K. Antony and found him Elizabeth, his wife. Both of them are Canara Bank employees. AK had decided against marriage but he once spoke of his loneliness to his bosom friend OC. His sole condition was that he would only marry in a registrar's office. It was agreed upon. The marriage took place at OC's Puthupally House in the presence of a sub registrar.

Made for Each Other

Kunju finds in Bava a source of prayerful power, the anchor of their family life. She gives him more love than he deserves, OC feels and he allows her, her personal freedom. Bava finds in Kunju an endless capacity for patience. He is not demanding or obstinate and never angry or plaintive. His voice is ever so soft and gentle, an excellent thing in men.

OC likes tapioca and fish. For supper, he would like to have porridge and green gram and for breakfast, steam cake with green gram or Bengal gram. He, however is not finicky and is content with whatever is served at table.

Bava manages their household affairs. OC hands over his salary to her. Education loan, vehicle loan, house loan, and others are all taken care of. Bava has had no complaints because her husband does not bring home tainted money.

Oommen Chandy has a special regard for his firstborn, Maria. Mariamma's pet however is neither her three children nor her grandchildren. But the 'youngest' of them all, and the gentlest, her Kunju!

Her only 'dear little one'!

Chronology

Birth date	:	31 October 1943
1961	:	President, Balajanasakyam
1965	:	State General Secretary, KSU
1967	:	State President, KSU
1969	:	State President, Youth Congress
1970	:	MLA
1977	:	MLA
March 1977 – Oct 78	:	Labour Minister
1980	:	MLA
Dec 1981 – March 82	:	Home Minister
1982	:	MLA
1982–85	:	UDF Convener
1987	:	MLA
1991	:	MLA
June 1991 – June 94	:	Finance Minister
1996	:	MLA
2001	:	MLA
2001–04	:	UDF Convener
Aug 2004 – May 06	:	Chief Minister
2006	:	MLA
Since 2006	:	Opposition Leader
Educational Qualification	:	BA, BL
Father	:	K. O. Chandy
Mother	:	Baby Chandy
Wife	:	Mariamma Oommen
Children	:	Maria, Achu, Chandy
Grandchildren	:	Ephi Noah, Angela Ann Philip